From Hairdressers to Pastors

From Hairdressers to Pastors

An Intergrative Approach to
Counseling and Connecting

James de Beer

HighWay
A division of Anomalos Publishing House
Crane

HighWay
A division of Anomalos Publishing House, Crane 65633
© 2009 by James de Beer
All rights reserved. Published 2009
Printed in the United States of America

09   1

ISBN-10: 0982036191 (paper)
EAN-13: 9780982036198 (paper)

A CIP catalog record for this book is available from the Library of Congress.

Cover illustration and design by Steve Warner

Contents

Acknowledgments

It would be so convenient if one could simply settle debt through a few words. It would surely have made this word of thanks much easier.

Nevertheless, I want to use this opportunity to express my sincere appreciation to my wife Margie for her wonderful support and kindness from the beginning, when writing the manuscript was only a thought.

A huge thanks to everyone involved for their input and suggestions.

To Graham, this book would not have been possible without your unselfish and persistent help and guidance.

And to all the staff of Anomalos, a special thanks for turning the manuscript into a publication.

Counseling and Connecting— a Handbook

People from all walks of life suffer more and more from fear, trauma, grief, and loss. Needs in the community are growing to breathtaking proportions. Those in need are searching for comfort, hoping to find it from those who are prepared to make themselves available for a chat, a cup of tea, or a moment to connect and share either some joyful laughter or sad and painful experiences.

I have always had a good head of hair. During a visit to New Zealand for my stepdaughter's wedding, I was expected to have a real father's haircut. My god-given, curly mop has always drawn me towards a hair salon rather than a barber. This time was no different. It did not take many seconds for the hairdresser to start a conversation with, "Are you from this area?" Some moments later she knew almost my whole pedigree, and in learning that I was a counselor, she posed the real McCoy. "I have a client who was diagnosed with terminal cancer. She told me this when she visited me yesterday; I didn't really know what to do or say to her. How should I handle her next time she comes in?" The question silenced me for a moment, thinking about the many opportunities for the hairdresser to be available in the life of someone searching for new meaning. Suddenly a twenty-minute haircut felt more like twenty seconds. I knew that there was so much to share.

Establishing a new identity for such a person, whether newly diagnosed with cancer, or some other catastrophic change in life, depends more on the way she is treated by others than by her own reactions to other treatments.

"She trusts you," I softly said. "Listen to her story while you do her hair. Use this quality time to be with her while she is dealing with it." We talked around the factor of "being," as opposed to "giving," an opinion. Every now and then, I noticed the hairdresser's changing facial expressions in the mirror as she thought about what it would be like to listen to someone, rather than sharing one-sided opinions and babbling all the time. I was aware that the client would probably be dealing with one, or at times more than one, phase of denial, detachment, anger, or grief associated with her illness.

A few minutes later, with a new look and a well-groomed haircut, I made my way to the counter to settle my bill. The hairdresser leaned closer and thanked me. "You know, eh? We get a lot of people here who talk about personal things. You have made me think about this thing of just being there and to—yeah, maybe listen more to their stories. I will give it a go, and we'll talk about it again next time you visit."

Not only did I leave with a well-groomed haircut, but I believe a seed was planted, and I know her mind was fertile; the mirror did not lie!

While this is only one story in the life of a person in need, existing governmental and private initiatives together just cannot cope with the load of many others. Caregivers often find themselves with a need for respite and government apportion money, as if that would solve the problems. The need for help spreads from substance abuse, domestic violence, eating disorders, financial problems, and family and couple problems to a variety of psychological stresses. Sadly, there is no end to the list. Where will these people end up if the willing and supportive few don't open their hearts and set aside time for them?

Has our disconnectedness from community led to the big "Self," or has our big "I" led to our disconnecting from community? Environmentalists and psychologists claim that focusing on "I" leads people to feel less connected to nature. They claim further that the heightened objective of self-awareness has been shown to increase self-focus and, therefore, a decrease in connection with nature and probably community results. The self and its feelings become our only moral guide. Our values become mutable, resulting in a lack of moral obligations. Instead of acting out of goodness, we become obsessed with self-gratification. While the self first seeks to determine its own form of action by searching for happiness, it separates from family, responsibility, respect, religion, ethics, and morals.

In 2003, an Australian wrote a letter to one of the Australian newspapers hoping to initiate some kind of "neighbor day," when people can connect, greet one another, and do someone a favor. This initiative was since shared with the then Australian head of state and other politicians with the hope of gaining support for a national Neighbor Day. During 2006, the United Nations (UN) extended an invitation for further discussions in New York with the purpose of this initiative becoming an official UN observance. Recently, a local pastor included in one of his weekly church bulletins the news that, "The body of a man has been found up to one year after his lonely death in the bedroom of his Sydney public housing unit, police say." He added, "This news headline caught my attention and moved my heart deeply." Have we really disconnected from community and other relationships to the degree that we now require a UN representative to introduce us to our neighbors so we can greet and communicate one day of the year? What about the other 364 days?

Another major concern in modern life is the lack of business ethics, which has resulted in people plundering into high levels of financial debt. Research has shown that several aspects of credit take advantage of people's cognitive and behavioral vulnerabilities. A 2002 medical paper links credit card debt to various health and social problems such as insomnia, anxiety, marital breakdowns, and depression.

Domestic violence has also reached new record highs, with social and health consequences. These consequences include anxiety, depression, emotional and physical stress symptoms, substance abuse, suicide, reduced coping skills, loss of self esteem, breakdown of relationships, and living in fear and other major impacts on quality of life. Children of perpetrators and victims fall into behavioral problems like poor adjustment and poor social competence, bullying, and family conflict. Lack of social skills often leads to bad financial management, eating disorders, and sometimes to a total lack of responsibility and self-respect. As mentioned earlier, the list goes on and on. It seems never-ending, and in many cases behaviors and experiences are intertwined.

The topics discussed and written about in this handbook have been identified as a number of the top pressing issues confronted by western societies in the 21st century. They are not placed into specific priorities or in some kind of value order but rather in a format that brings out a great variety of commonly used theories, practices, and therapeutic techniques to address certain needs of people.

I am aware that this handbook only addresses a limited area, but I am positive that each one of us can make a difference. It is through individual connectedness, as well as collective community compact, that we have the strength to turn our societies around in a way that we can model goodness onto our loved ones, friends, and neighbors.

This handbook is dedicated to counselors, teachers, hairdressers, school principles, pastors, elders, community and church leaders, human resource practitioners, people in need, doctors, business owners, health workers, executive managers, neighbors, students, and those who have the gifts of mercy and love.

If you feel like connecting with someone in need, or you are the connector, or if you know someone in need, you are invited to take the step and get them this book—don't just recommend it. Mere talk does not always bear fruit. By doing this you already show that you are being genuine—an ingredient necessary for relationship building.

Chapter One

Influences on the Experience of Disability

Unfortunately there are no simple answers. Understanding and intervening within the experience of illness and disability goes well beyond just the physiological description of a medical condition, diminished capacity, or the aging process. We will focus on the experience of illness, disability or aging, the various influences on this experience, and the challenges these influences present for those who care for such people. We will also be concerned with those who provide such care within the constraints of existing social and health systems.

The Experience of Disability

So what is the experience of disability for individuals faced with health and capacity issues? What understanding is there of the physical, psychological, social, cultural, and spiritual influences of the experience? What are the implications for formal and informal caregivers of how a person actually experiences such a condition? This discussion will endeavor to incorporate understanding of the constraints on care that recognizes the total experience of disability and reduced capacity.

The visibility of impairments, the perceptions and concepts of normality, the personal experience of disability, the effects of degraded environments, and the ever-escalating health interventions for the elderly all contribute to the awareness of disability. It spans the boundaries of academia, personal experience, and political, social, economic, environmental, medical, psychosocial, and public policy. While there are heated debates in both the disability studies literature and the popular press over the experience, meanings, context, and consequences of disability, fundamentally disability is defined by public policy and therefore disability is whatever policy says it is. This concept does not specify whether the problem is located in the individual or in the environment, it only represents an official belief that a disability constitutes a disadvantage. Smith and Smith (1991), however, go one step further in stating that legislation is only an expression of intent backed by the authority of the law concerned. The question remains, how is this intent translated into practice? Action to achieve purpose is therefore the key issue.

This idea of institutionalized discrimination against disabled people has been used to argue for anti-discrimination policies that focus on change in behavior rather than attitudes. Hence, studies reflect a significant attempt to narrow the gap between disability as a social construct and disability as a social creation. The actual experience of ill people, according to Hahn (1986, 132), "has been conspicuously absent in most previous investigations of the issue."

Experience, interpretation of meaning, and its consequences, can differ markedly across individuals. The personal experience of the person and interpretation of the meaning of the illness or disability cannot be assumed. Judith Murray uses an example in which an elderly man with osteoporosis, internal circulation problems, and having little social support or mobility is compared with a sixteen-year-old male who, in contrast, is physically fit and whose mother can give support at home. Should both have suffered from a broken leg, in most cases it would be anticipated that the sixteen-year-old male would heal more quickly; not necessarily so. Past experience in the life of the elderly man may help him to handle the broken leg as a minor injury whereas the younger man could be an athlete in the peak of his performance, in which case the injury could end his dreams of becoming a national sportsman.

Smith and Smith (1991, 44) state that "the experience will be different for those who were born disabled than for those who became disabled later in life." Moving from non-disabled to a disabled condition demands a number of adaptations by the person concerned. Depending on the nature of the impairment, the healing process can at times be a lengthy one regardless of whether the onset was sudden or insidious, or whether the impairment's effects were progressive or static. Personal assumptions about oneself, one's place in society, one's family, and one's skills and abilities are suddenly the subject of reappraisal, sometimes dictated by others.

Influences on the Experience of Disability

The process of establishing a new identity for the person who becomes disabled, rather than being born disabled, is being influenced by many factors, more so by the way they are treated by the non-disabled or their own reactions to the treatment. Too many people still view a disabled person as a cripple in the old, pitying, derogatory sense, not only in body but in mind.

Assumptions on the part of the non-disabled can falsely color the identity that the impaired person is developing. Cerebral palsy and deafness are two conditions in which it is often assumed that there must inevitably be some negative effects to the disabled person's mental or effective functioning. An implicit assumption is that, because of their disability, they are not whole persons and that they are incapable of functioning in other areas of their lives. On one hand the disability is being interpreted as a total handicap, while on the other hand disabled people feel that they are normal in all aspects except in one small area of their life. In crossing the threshold from a non-disabled to a disabled condition, the traumatic experience responsible for the event is vividly remembered in very fine detail by the person. Having dealt with denial, detachment, anger, and grief associated with the disability, the person then has to start trying to build a new identity. This is a learning process needing to accept limitations and to move back into normality, however far away normality is.

Boazman (1999, 18–19) describes his experience of professionals, when he became aphasic after a stroke, as follows: "Their responses towards me varied greatly, some showed great compassion, while others showed complete indifference. I had no way of communicating the fact that I was a bright, intelligent, whole human being. That is what hurt the most."

Disabled people have found that health and caring professionals impinge on other and wider aspects of their lives. The *medicalization* of their lives seem to impact on matters such as decisions made on their behalf relating to employment, education, social benefits, and other pertinent issues. Many medical professionals have viewed disabled people as tragic, deficient, and inferior and have sought to eliminate them through institutionalization, and to cure or approximate them to normal through surgery, drugs, and rehabilitation. The power to assess disabled people, to define their needs, control their resources, specify solutions, and evaluate outcomes can be used or abused as the opportunity lies in the hands of the health and medical profession. This power base, together with a disabling physical and social environment, has kept disabled people in a dependent position within society. When the descriptions of the reality of disabled people are not understood, and psychiatric labels are imposed, their sense of self can be disrupted and this, in turn, can be very distressing to them.

The medical model, according to Corker and Shakespeare (2002), tends to explain disability universally and ends up creating totalizing meta-historical narratives that exclude critical components of disabled people's lives, knowledge, and experience. The global experience of people with impairments is too complex to be rendered within one unitary model or set of ideas. Not too distant from this school of thought is how Smith and Smith (1991) describe the way we currently define disability. It relies on a medical model for expression. Invariably, a person with a disability starts along the medical road and is forced into adopting a sick role. Although society accords special privileges to this role, it also becomes a label which implies membership of a non-healthy group.

A practicing doctor writes that he was horrified looking back on what he imagined to be the experience of a disabled person, which he encountered during the time that he was a non-disabled physician. Now, fifteen years after becoming disabled, he finds himself totally at home with the concept of just being who he really is. Bassnet (2001, 453) stated, "Now I know that my assessment of the potential quality of life of severely disabled people was clearly flawed." In another example, Spence's experience is related by Mitchell and Snyder (1997, 63) as "explaining my experience as a patient (mastectomy) and the contradictions between [this experience and] ways in which the medical profession controls women's bodies and the imaginary bodies we inhabit as women."

Any social model of disability is about social change. This is described as the vision of the liberation and emancipation of the disabled by developing collective and individual critical consciousness. This approach is to change the lives of the disabled through changing the disabled environment, prejudicial attitudes, and unequal power relations which exclude them from participatory citizenship. Despite the objective reality, what becomes a disability is determined by social meanings people attach to particular physical and mental impairments. This concept does not seek to specify whether the problem is located in the person or in the environment. The term *social death* describes the experience of many people who have undergone what they feel to be a social rejection of their bodies to the point of withdrawal from society.

Challenges for Caregivers

Caregivers of those who are less than able face enormous challenges. The experience of spinal injury for instance cannot be understood in terms of purely internal, psychological, or interpersonal processes. It incorporates a whole range of material factors such as housing, finance, employment, and family circumstances, which can and will change over time, sometimes for better and sometimes for worse. Caregivers are not necessarily divorced from these circumstances. Difficult circumstances make both physical and mental suffering worse and harder to bear. These factors are likely to cause error, but not as much as the ignorance and fear of those who have little or no experience of being disabled.

Although disability is relative to a person's physical, social, and cultural environment, the availability and distribution of basic resources such as water, food, clothing, and shelter have major effect on the experience of the disabled (Wendell 1996).

Some researchers hold the view that neither a psychological nor a social-psychological approach provides an adequate account of the experience of disability. Thus, disabled people need not be labeled less than human but rather ordinary people coping with extraordinary circumstances.

As in a medical and social perspective, there are hundreds of definitions pertaining to the cultural perspective of disability. However, Stone (2005) argues that in his definition of culture there are two key components that culture is first learned and then shared. Culture should be viewed as a system consisting of principal elements such as normative codes (ways of behaving), communication codes (verbal and non-verbal), knowledge (necessary information), problem-solving strategies, relationships, and methods of transmitting culture to young and new members of the cultural group. From this context, anyone who is removed out of the domain of these elements will have a different experience. Feelings of abandonment may be strong as a result of the presence of a different culture. Changes to the configuration of families may be disruptive and lead to negative personal experiences and violate values and beliefs.

The physical body is invested with cultural meaning and the social experience that could be expected from individuals. The fact that in recent years there has been a growing recognition that some dominant cultural images of the disabled (as portrayed in the arts, media, and literature) not only violate the actual experience, but are also unhelpful in breaking down prejudice. In presenting the disabled person as less than or more than human—this phenomenon is commonly referred to as the "generalized other." The crucial significant other in the lives of the disabled is that vast array of professionals who either write things about or do things to disabled people. These professionals' world views, heavily influenced by the medical model, reinforce the less than human cultural image of the disabled.

In the world of disabled people the word "independence" has more than one meaning. This can lead to great confusion. The core fact is that we are all dependent on one another for some physical, social and emotional needs. Yet there is that side of a person that can be defined as any set of ideas which focuses on the individual and the individual's interests. In a narrow sense, physical self-reliance is generally considered to be something that disabled people desire above all, however inefficient, frustrating, and stressful it may be. The experience of being able to dress and wash oneself, walk, clean the house, and make the bed are critical regardless of the time taken. The ability to be in control, from a personal psychological point of view, lies within the individual's experience and coping mechanisms such as acceptance of the disability, self-concept, level of control, spirituality, sexuality, intelligence, and adaptability. Although disabled people are usually regarded as the recipients of care, the notion of interdependency applies to them as much as to anyone else. As strange as it might seem, during the Second World War when jobs were plentiful, more disabled people were in open employment only to lose it when the war was over (Humphries and Gordon 1992).

It is almost impossible to end these comments without another experienced story. For about three years after being hit by a car and suffering severe head injuries, Colin Cameron did not consider being anything other than normal. It was later that he finally came to understand that being normal was not an option anymore and that he resented being defined by schoolmates and teachers as the poor boy who had the accident. He wanted to be known as something else, and his own way of managing this was to become very bitter and cynical. He found that he was labeled either as a sad, pathetic victim or a tragic but brave hero. Yet his lived experience of impairment was much more complicated than that. He had the desire to define himself and to search for a new identity—to come out as disabled.

Morris believes that the assumption that disabled people want to be normal rather than just as they are is one the most oppressive experiences. "I want to be able to celebrate my difference, not hide from it." There is a growing belief that any abnormality demonstrated by disabled people results not from their impairment, but from the failure of society to meet their normal needs (Swain et al. 2003, 83).

The most important experiences of a physical disability are the psychological and social adjustment with which the individual struggles. Not all disabilities involve disfigurement, but all physical disabilities that result in long-term loss of mobility will impact on the view the person has about him or herself. An individual's body image is the mental picture of him or herself. This includes the physical self, appearance, sexual attractiveness, and skills. More important is how the person with a disability is viewed by others. This we should never forget.

References

Barnes, C., M. Oliver, and L. Barton, eds. 2002. *Disability studies today.* Cornwell: MPG Books.

Basnett, I. 2001. Health care professionals and their attitudes towards and decisions affecting disabled people. *Handbook of disability studies.* London: Sage.

Boazman, S. 1999. Inside aphasia. In *Disability discourse.* Buckingham: Open University Press.

Corker, M., and S. French, eds. 1999. *Disability discourse.* Buckingham: Open University Press.

Corker, M., and T. Shakespeare. 2002. *Disability and post-modernity: Embodying disability theory.* London: Continuum.

Hahn, H. 1986. Public support for rehabilitation programs: The analysis of U.S. disability policy. *Disability, Handicap, and Society* 1:132.

Hancock, P., B. Hughes, E. Jagger, K. Paterson, R. Russel, E. Tulle-Winton, and M. Tyler. 2000. *The Body, culture and society: An introduction.* Buckingham: Open University Press.

Humphries, S., and P. Gordon. 1992. *Out of sight: The experience of disability 1900–1950.* Plymouth: Northcote House.

McLaren, P., and P. Leonard. 1993. *Paulo freire: A critical encounter.* London: Routledge.

Mead, G. H. 1934. *Mind, self and society: From the standpoint of a social behaviourist.* Chicago: University of Chicago Press.

Mitchell, D. T., and S. L. Snyder, eds. 1997. *The body and physical difference: Discourses of disability.* Ann Arbor: The University of Michigan Press.

Murray, J. 2002. Communicating with the community about grieving: A description and a review of the foundations of the broken leg analogy of grieving. *Journal of Loss and Trauma* 7:47–69.

Oliver, M. 1990. *The politics of disablement.* Houndmills: McMillian.

Robinson Jr., F. M., D. West, and D. Woodworth Jr. 1995. *Coping+plus: Dimensions of disability.* Greenwood: USA.

Shearer, A. 1981. *Disability: whose handicap?* Oxford: Blackwell.

Smart, J. 2001. *Disability: Society and the individual.* Austin: Pro. Ed.

Smith, N. J., and H. C. Smith. 1991. *Physical disability and handicap: A social work approach.* Kuala Lumpur: Percetakan Anda Sdn.

Stone, J. H., ed. 2005. *Culture and disability: Providing culturally competent services.* Thousand Oaks: Sage.

Swain, J., S. French, and C. Cameron. 2003. *Controversial issues in a disabling society.* Buckingham: Open University Press.

Wendell, S. 1996. *The rejected body: Feminist philosophical reflections on disability.* New York: Routledge.

Chapter Two

Theories of Counseling

Although the exact number is not clear, there are some 220-plus existing counseling theories. While this scenario might paint a picture of confusion, there is a common thread among them all. It offers a way of being heard and of being known. A theory helps us to explain events. It provides the counselor with structure in the face of chaos. It offers a client a way of making sense.

A theory is simply a systematically organized body of knowledge applicable in a relatively wide variety of circumstances, especially a system of assumptions, accepted principles, and rules of procedure devised to analyze, predict, or otherwise explain the nature or behavior of a specified set of phenomena. It is important to be aware of those aspects of theory that challenge one's frame of reference. This is critical in the application of theoretical practices relating to one's worldview, values, and experience. How the client may perceive the application of certain intervention practices is another crucial factor for the counselor.

People are complex. They can alternatively, through theoretical metaphors, be reflected as mechanistic, social, spiritual, and more. Our social background, culture, history, and individual experiences are different, while our imagination is our reality. Who we are and how we see things will determine how we will construct our life experiences. This is as relevant to the counselor as it is to any other person. It is then necessary to critically look and reflect on counseling theories and the impact they have on the personal development of the counselor. How we intervene will determine the transformation of the construct. Thus, we need to understand the importance of selecting the theory and approach that will be best for the client in a specific situation. Therefore, one single theory cannot be *the* only way. However, it may be *a* way and in the face of chaos and complexity a theory can act as a tool for communicating reflection on experience, which will determine the change and transformation required.

Psychoanalytic Therapy: The Talking Cure

Psychoanalysis as the talking cure has grown from Sigmund Freud's perspective as a qualified physician and his way of being was from a neutral position holding back from the client. The therapist represents him or herself as a *blank screen* and from this neutral position works with the client to make the unconscious, conscious. As McLeod (2003, 83) describes this phenomenon: "to get the ego where id was." This process is known as *transference*, where the client reflects on to the therapist earlier experiences; and *counter transference* if the therapist responds and discloses earlier personal experiences in a similar way.

Freud's five *stages of development,* namely oral, anal, phallic, latency, and genital remain popular tools in contemporary counseling development theories. His *topography of the mind,* i.e., ego, super ego, and id still remain the building blocks of understanding people's behavior. Another aspect is that of *defense mechanisms* of which *repression* is the cornerstone on which the structure of psychoanalysis is built. To keep things repressed is hard work and can lead to neurotic misperceptions, misinterpretations, and inappropriate behavior.

Much of Freud's theory of psychoanalysis is claimed to be somewhat based on his personal opinion and writings that are difficult to get meaning from. Furthermore, much of his theory lacks scientific proof.

Nevertheless, Freud's theory of psychoanalysis has great value. It helps in understanding, especially in the fields of childhood and early life development, ego topography of mind, and how defense mechanisms can naturally be applied. How one, as counselor, can be neutral and detached, especially in the spheres of emotional and irrational worlds, is a question yet to be fully answered. However, the deep and secret world of people is very different from the *worried well.* The exploration of people's secret world differentiates psychoanalysis from other theories, such as CBT and post-modern psychotherapy in general. From a theory perspective, Freud remains the father of psychotherapy, and psychoanalysis is the foundation thereof.

Psychodynamic Theory: Psychoanalysis Evolving

The beginning of the evolving of psychoanalysis was the splitting from Freud by theorists such as Jung, Ferenczi, Rank, Reich, Adler, and others. The ways of being, understanding, and intervention were viewed from different paradigms. The concepts of *anxiety* and *safety* (Jung 1968) gave new meaning to psychotherapy and a new foundation to psychodynamics. Questions such as "How do unconscious processes and mechanisms operate?" and

"What technique is the most effective?" required research and answers beyond psychoanalytic therapy.

While psychoanalysis focuses on id, intrapsychic, defenses, and biological factors, the psychodynamic school focuses on ego, interpersonal, mastery, adaptation, and social factors. The work of Adler as a psychosocial analyst gave rise to the first occupational health and safety workbook as well as foundational input to child clinics, family work, women's rights, parenthood, worker's rights, and equal relationships. He approached such issues from a common sense point of view and was criticized for it. This school of thought was different from the psychoanalytical view in that the client was seen as one in a relationship as a social being. The hallmark of Adler was not from a medical, but from an encouragement of people perspective. His approach was that social and psychological support would get rid of inferiority. This was to find the optimal level of the self and the client's worldview based on earlier family structure and future dreams.

The influences of Karen Horney that the individual requires a safe and secure environment, that the past is the past, was future focused. Through a therapeutic relationship of trust, respect, and help one could find the actual self. Her basic strategies were to move towards people that are helpless, to stand up against aggressiveness, and to detach oneself from such situations. Also influential was the school of object-relations such as Melanie Klein's school of the relationship between mothers and their children during the first few months. The quality of the relationship sets patterns for later-life behavior.

John Bowlby's attachment theory, at the front of contemporary research, is based on aspects such as biological function of intimate emotional bonds between people. Primary to this is the child's development of the ways the child is treated by parents, and especially the mother. Psychotherapy is seen as corrective therapy to those who distrust the world and who do not have the ability to identify what, where, and who they are in the world. The world is seen as a place of relationships (McLeod 2003). Important are the four types of attachment, namely:

1. Secure/feeling and dealing;
2. Insecure/resistant, i.e., feeling but not dealing;
3. Insecure/avoidant, i.e., dealing but not feeling;
4. Disorganized/disoriented attachment, i.e., not feeling and not dealing.

The therapeutic relationship is one of creating a safe and secure environment for the client. This will allow the client to explore various unhappy and painful aspects of life. Past or present experiences can only be explored in a trusted relationship with a companion during transference and counter transference psychotherapy.

The emphasis on psycho-socio, object relational, and attachment aspects has surely brought a new perspective to classic psychoanalysis. It adds to the school of psychotherapy more options to the counselor as well as the client.

Person-Centered Theory: Rogerian Therapy

Person-centered psychotherapy is the humanistic approach to prize the person. It is the common knowledge approach and holds a view of positive regard. Rogers, influenced by Adler and Rank moved away from the medical perspective to that of personal growth. In a non-directive way clients redefine themselves and take control of their lives. Critical to the congruent relationship of necessary and sufficient conditions are the factors of unconditional positive regard for the client and an empathic approach reflected in feeling. Establishing rapport through listening and trusting the client reflects feeling, allows for free expression, and helps an individual to interact spontaneously. The acceptance that the client knows the past, has a picture of the future, and is valued as a human is core to successful therapy. The person-centered therapeutic model holds value in relationship rather than in a specific technique.

This therapeutic approach contributes a tremendous amount of value to counseling, not only in the sense of therapeutic alliance, but also in the sphere of humanity where both the counselor and the client have the opportunity to reflect authentic aspects of being. While being warm and trustworthy, one's own values can bring balance between separateness and connectedness. The counseling process plays out in the *here and now*. The most critical question is whether the counselor can be an authentic person and at the same time reveal such authenticity.

Gestalt Therapy

Gestalt therapy as a humanistic approach plays a large part in real life experience through figures, shapes, and patterns; simultaneously being at two places at the same time. Gestalt therapy is like being figurative in the foreground and background while focusing on the present moment rather than what was, might have been, could have been, or should be. Every person experiences the five layers of *being:*

1. Phony/not the real self
2. Phobic/fear of reaching the core of the person
3. Impasse/point of stop

4. Inclusive/painful development and no energy
5. The core/explosive

The essence of the counselor is seeing the client as *the most important*, looking at the *here and now*, and staying with questions such as *how and what*. While psychoanalysis is based on interpretation of information, Gestalt focuses on dialogue between counselor and client, which is in contrast to one another. Gestalt therapy is also based on relationship, feelings, and intuition. Nothing is less or more important, such as verbal or non-verbal communication and body language, and both counselor and client are responsible for themselves.

The client's awareness of feelings and thoughts in the moment are explored through the counseling relationship, not by means of a specific technique. Dialogue between counselor and client is about talking to one another. It is the ability to make contact with people and the environment, playing out dreams and life experiences through role-play with the empty chair, and experiencing real emotion. While existential and experiential therapy is the essence of Gestalt therapy, it is a therapy to help clients realize unfinished business.

Gestalt therapy can be extremely useful to play out troublesome experiences *at the moment* of feeling it or thinking (cognitive) of it. *Experiential* moments are more reliable than interpretation. It allows one to take off the mask and find the real self. As in person-centered therapy, the value of Gestalt therapy lies in the here and now.

Cognitive-Behavioral Therapy (CBT)

CBT is one of the most widely used counseling approaches. CBT is a therapeutic school that stands in contrast to psychoanalysis, other psychodynamic therapies, and Gestalt therapy. It is not about feelings, emotions, relationships, and systems; it is about what you think. The emphasis is on the thought process. It works directly against the client's feelings and disturbances. CBT is based on the premise that our thoughts cause our feelings and behaviors. We can therefore change the way we think, in turn, to feel better even though we might not be able to change the situation.

The rational approach to things that causes emotional upset to people is due to unrealistic beliefs in a school of thought that works well with rational thinking people. Ignoring the deeper feelings of people seems irrational and that, in itself, becomes invalidated. Therefore the ABCDEF of Ellis and the common distortions that a cognitive therapist should listen for in client's stories can only successfully be applied in therapeutic intervention to clients that have a similar belief system. Self-directed learning by a client can overcome negative interpretations and views. Recent work on CBT has argued that rationalism could lead to constructivism, which acknowledges the past. Deeper core beliefs and contemporary CBT is evolving into an integrative school of counseling. Yet questions arise whether irrational thoughts can allow one to spiral down into depression, or whether self-directed learning can help transform positive images.

Existential Theory of Counseling

The existential theory of counseling was derived from the philosophical work of Victor Frankl (Cooper 2003) in the domain of logotherapy (people with hope and purpose). It states that being in the world brings new meaning to concepts such as love, death, anxiety, suffering, freedom, isolation, and meaninglessness. Existential theory further holds that for people to live their lives in full, they need capacity for self-awareness, freedom, and responsibility. They search for meaningful relationships, purpose, values, and goals. It claims that anxiety is a condition of living. There is also an awareness of non-being in the world. This physical world (umwelt) helps us to relate to our environment and the natural world around us. Other influential factors such as our attitudes to our own bodies, our surroundings, the climate, and material possessions play roles in this physical world. In our social world (mitwelt), we interact with others in the greater public arena. In our private world (eigenwelt), we create a personal, private, and psychological domain for ourselves. The spiritual world (uber-welt) allows us the creation of an ideal world. These concepts describe how people live in different worlds at the same time.

The primary aspect of Frankl's theory is therapy through finding meaning. It is to strive for something. Also that tension is necessary for health, unlike psychodynamics where the purpose of therapy is to reduce tension. The way of being in a therapeutic relationship is to lead, help, and support the client to find new meaning in life. This is seen as a privileged position for the counselor to be engaged in.

Understanding that the person is in a process of *becoming* (growth) and not in a static position with set traits can bring help to the mass neurotic triad of depression, addiction, and aggression. These characteristic behaviors cover a huge portion of society which leads to anxiety disorders, obsessive-compulsive disorder, depression, and schizophrenia. Meaning can be found through experiencing something we value and through creative values such as doing something good for one's neighbor. Suffering and attitude add to ways through which one can find meaning along paths such as altruism, dedication to cause, creativity, religion, and self-growth.

The therapeutic process of existential therapy is searching for the value and meaning in an individual's life by asking questions such as the following:

What do you want?
What are you experiencing right now?
Who are you?
Who do you want to be?
Who are you choosing to be?
What do you want to say right now?

This theory can be combined with person-centered, Gestalt, CBT, psychodynamics, and other schools of humanistic, behavioral, and post-modern theories. It also gives meaning to people as humans and values them as being in this world. To experience something, to put one's mind into gear, and to direct for meaning can surely result in successful outcome.

Narrative Therapy: A Post-Modern Theory

The post-structural approach of narrative therapy is what distinguishes itself from other psychotherapies. Michael White's outline on narrative therapy is that it can be difficult to communicate as we speak to other people in their *language*—one that they have been socialized in and have internalized. Thus, we construct our relationships through certain ways that contain us to stay true to these internalized stories. Therefore, every person has been through their own language discourse which includes the counselor as part of their language. Each individual's structural language represents a difference and is based on the following:

- Language represents, communicates, describes, is informative, and is neutral in its effects on people.
- It categorizes things into dualism: good/bad, success/failure, etc.
- It sees the core self as fixated by early experience and significant others.
- It sees the counselor is the expert.
- It uses interpretation as the central construct.
- It works through insight, history, beliefs, being responsible, and taking charge of destiny.

It is through discourse that our sense of who we are becomes unclear. Issues such as physical body, spiritual self, and mind's free will fade as our minds cloud. Therefore language is our discourse. It shapes us into certain positions and we can comply, resist, or flow with these relations of power.

Narrative questioning is based on structural internalizing conversations and post-structural language (externalizing or narrative conversations—stepping outside the problem and looking into it). From this paradigm the internal conversation refers to the problem as belonging to the person ("I am worried") and external conversation refers to the problem as being the problem ("It is worries that..."). Therefore problems are separated from people as we story our being into reality. The counselor intervenes through externalizing language to find an alternative story to that of pathology. Through thickening and deconstructing the language of the negative construction of truth, the counselor helps the client to make a stand and find a new way to the future. Stories help shape people's lives and relationships, and therefore meaning cannot be separated from experience. Thus stories give meaning to people's experience.

Aspects of narrative therapy can be seen in other theories such as CBT, Rational-Emotive Therapy (RET) and psychodynamic schools. However, it has its own framework of reference, which could be applied with successful counseling. The constructivist narrative therapy takes the client through a program consisting of different stages:

- Recalling the story, expressing their experience of life;
- Objectifying the story through interpretive acts;
- Subjectifying the story through interpretive acts;
- Finding new construction in the story in the language of the client.

This can perhaps take time and special effort with successful change in behavior.

Solution-Focused Therapy

Solution-focused therapy is often referred to as brief therapy. Its basic premise is a belief that people know more than they have been able to recall. While clients have *expertise* in their problems they rather focus on what they want to achieve. The role of the therapist is to evoke this knowledge through skilful questioning. The therapist must do the following:

- Profoundly respect the client's capacity to change;
- Respect the client for their beliefs to find solutions;

- Protect the client's integrity;
- Focus on exceptions and on what is already working;
- Avoid problem talk.

As a post-modern therapy, solution-focused therapy distinguishes itself from narrative therapy in that it is not focused on internalized issues. However, like narrative therapy it is focused on externalized language. The client-as-expert has a pre-identified goal and the focus is setting up this goal statement or desired outcome. In doing so, the therapist becomes the expert in asking questions, giving compliments to any small achievement, amplifying small changes, and looking for actions or incidents. Furthermore, the therapist focuses on things that work and poses scaling questions (such as on a scale of one to ten) from the least to the most important aspects of opinion on achievements and progress. Steering away from stereotyping, negative talk, the therapist works towards reframing events in terms of patterns, giving tasks, and posing the *miracle* question, "When you wake up in the morning knowing that a miracle has happened through the night, what do you think would have changed in your life?"

The therapist and the client then start working towards the identified preferred future.

The stages of solution-building can be described as developing and transforming the therapist-client relationship. This is done by identifying well-formed goals (small, concrete, and important), giving compliments at the end of session, and evaluating the client's progress.

Counseling for solutions in a brief therapy session seems just too simplistic. It creates the impression that this therapy was written for insurance companies. However, being positive about life in general can do many people well.

Christian Counseling

There appears to be two distinctive approaches under the umbrella of *Christian Counseling*. On the one hand, there is the school commonly referred to as the "Adams" model. This model also known as *Nouthetic Counseling*, or *Biblical Counseling*, rejects the need for psychological intervention because the "Word of God" is the only valid authority (Adams 1986). On the other end of the scale, there is the school of thought known as Christian Counseling. This school in some degree and form allows for other theories to be integrated, which is best explained within behavioral, cognitive, and Freudian models.

Behavioral. Environmental and psychological aspects are seen as interference, and that man can change as the Holy Spirit works within him. Although the environment has great influence on man's behavior and making changes in the environment may be useful in counseling, it is man's relationship with God through language that is pivotal. While man and animal live in the same environment and breathe the same air, the man-God relationship marks him as different. From this perspective, the gifts required for biblical counseling are exactly those that God has given to the biblical counselor, with the Bible as *God's Word* and guidance.

Cognitive. This model allows for combined psychological insights and participation of mental health professionals. It also makes provision and room for the influence of the Holy Spirit. It is based on the Biblical writings of Romans 12:2, "Do not conform any longer to the pattern of this world, but be transformed by the renewing of your mind" (New International Version).

Freudian. The Freudian school assumes that people's problems derive from past experiences. Here God's presence is invoked to work with past traumatic experiences. The role of the counselor is merely to facilitate prayer, "with Jesus, who replaces lies associated with past traumas with his truth" (Garner 2003, 8). The role and function of meditation as well as hypnosis have been described as examples of very active therapy where theology and anthropology can intertwine.

If psychology offers insights that will sharpen the counselor's skills and increase effectiveness, it would be beneficial to know and use them. There is a vast volume of literature out there that should be tapped into. Crabb writes that creating a wall between Scripture and psychology must be rejected.

Unlike other counseling schools, Christian counselors depart from the point of working with the client in his or her totality, i.e., spiritually, mentally, physically, and emotionally. For Christian counselors to achieve their goals they must apply the same basic interpersonal skills as all other counselors such as listening, reflecting feeling, showing authentic interest, and building on a therapeutic relationship.

People need meaning, purpose, and love. They need to feel secure and valued as persons. Many personal problems result from a deficit in one, or at times, in all of these needs. While the Lord Jesus Christ is completely sufficient to fully meet these needs, His power and authority are channeled through Christian counselors in their endeavors to provide help and support.

Integrative Therapy

Research over the thirty years since 1975 has shown that various psychotherapy theories reflect little or no differences. These findings actually highlight the Dodo Bird Effect in that everyone has won and all must have prizes.

Although the *battle of the brands* is over, there are still some psychotherapy schools and individual practicing therapists that are strongly committed to a particular theory. Yet there is no evidence that one is more effective than the other. There are basically two similarities to all theories: namely ideas about the process of change; and secondly, the role of interventions. What is furthermore important to acknowledge is the value and the role that research play in therapeutic practices, and that there is no ideological purity to one specific approach.

There are four specific areas to integrative therapy. The first area is that of *common factors,* which determines the core elements that different therapies share in common. The second area is the *technical element* designed to improve the counselor's ability to select the best treatment for the client. The third area is *theoretical integration* in which two or more therapies are integrated during the same counseling process. The last area to integrative therapy is the incorporation of *ideas and strategies* by counselors from other sources into their counseling practice.

Regardless of therapy, the client values the therapist's personality as important to the relationship and outcome. Helping the client to understand the problem, encouraging the client, and making oneself available to talk to are factors that the client values as being important to a successful outcome. The best approach is the one that will fit the client and the circumstances at the moment that the client is in need of therapy. Additional factors have been identified as common to the therapeutic process and the outcome which, in short, are the following:

- Extra therapeutic factors that determine change account for some 40 percent success;
- The therapeutic relationship account for some 30 percent success;

- Client expectancy (placebo effect) 15 percent;
- Theory or technique 15 percent.

Also important to the integrative model are the common factors identified, in that people are subjectively incompetent, distressed, and demoralized, and that they are therefore sad, anxious, hopeless, and lack self esteem. The basic principle in all forms of therapy is the same. It is a corrective emotional experience suitable to repair the traumatic influence of previous experiences. Carl Rogers emphasized a relationship that reflected empathy, congruence, and positive regard.

Combining two or more theories for maximum clinical effectiveness for lifestyle behaviors such as drinking, smoking, and drug abuse are referred to as *Transtheoretical Models of Change* (TTM) and consist of dimensions namely processes, stages, and levels.

Process. During the therapeutic process there is an attempt to raise the client's consciousness through goal-setting, giving direction, and working on self-evaluation (inside-out), environment evaluation (outside-in), and self-liberation, which may lead to change. From a behavioral therapy paradigm reinforcing self-management, controls all stimuli and works on counter conditioning. From a person-centered school there is emphasis on the relationship that may lead to emotional relief and change.

Stages. The first stage starts where the client believes that he or she does not have a problem (precontemplation). The next step follows when the client contemplates and prepares to be cognitively involved. Then the therapist helps the client to take action and maintain a mode of problem solving. Finally the session is terminated with successful outcome and change.

Levels. Thus, the client has tasks and needs and if the client wants to spend time on change it is important that the client identifies the problem by looking back to what has, or what has not, worked for the client in the past. This is crucial, as the client cannot stay in an emotional realm forever.

Understanding the integrative school one must accept that there is no single theory for all clients and all problems. There must also be recognition to therapeutic commonalities and identification of specific treatments of choice. The ultimate question in this model then is: What therapeutic approach is best for the person and his or her problem in front of the therapist?

References

Adams, J. E. 1986. *The Christians counselor's manual: The practice of nouthetic counseling.* Grand Rapids: Zondervan.

Beck, A. T. 1979. *Cognitive therapy and the emotional disorders.* New York: Penguin Books.

Bohart, A. C., and K. Tallman. 1999. *How clients make therapy work: The process of active self-healing.* Washington, DC: American Psychological Association.

Bowlby, J. 1999. *Attachment and loss.* New York: Basic Books.

Collins, G. R. 1988. *Christian counseling: A comprehensive guide.* New York: W. Publishing Group.

Cooper, M. 2003. *Existential therapies.* London: Sage Publications.

Crabb Jr, L. J. 1977. *Effective biblical counseling.* Grand Rapids: Zondervan Publishing House.

De Shazer, S. 1988 *Clues: Investigating solutions in brief therapy.* W. W. Norton and Co.

Duncan, B. L., and S. D. Miller. 2000. The client's theory of change: Consulting the client in the integrative process. *Journal of Psychotherapy Integration 10(2):*169–187.

Frankl, V. 1997. *Man's search for meaning.* Pocket.

Garner, G. 2003. *Christian models of counseling: Just a secular model.* Bible College of Queensland.

Gay, P. 1988. *Freud: A life for our time.* London: J.M. Dent.

George, E., C. Iveson, and H. Ratner. 1990. *Problem to solution: Brief therapy with individuals and families.* BT Press.

Jung, C. G. 1968. The psychology of the child archetype. In *The collected works of C. G. Jung (Vol 9).* Princeton, NJ: Princeton University Press.

Lax, B. 1999. Definition of narrative therapy. *A report presented at dulwich centre*. Adelaide, Australia.

McLeod, J. 2003. *An introduction to counseling*. Maidenhead: Open University Press.

Norcross, J. C., and M. R. Goldfried. 2005. *Handbook of psychotherapy integration*. New York: Oxford.

Parloff, M. B. 1986. Jerome Frank's common elements in psychotherapy: Non-specific factors and placebos. *American Journal of Orthopsychiatry* 56(4): 521–533.

Perls, F. 1969. *Gestalt therapy verbatim*. Lafayette, CA: Real People Press.

Rogers, C. R. 1980. *A way of being*. Boston: Houghton Mifflin.

Wampold, B. E. 2001. *The great psychotherapy debate: Models, methods, and findings*. Mahwah, NJ: Lawrence Erlbaum.

Westbrook, D., H. Kennerley, and J. Kirk. 2007. *An introduction to cognitive behavior therapy: Skills and applications*. London: Sage Publications.

White, M. 1997. Narrative therapy outline. *A report presented at the Dulwich Centre*. Adelaide, Australia.

Chapter Three

Domestic Violence

SECTION ONE:
Understanding the Causes of Domestic and Family Violence

Understanding the causes of domestic and family violence and how it relates to our interventions is the main focus of this chapter. Further emphasis is on the understanding of standards of practice and effective intervention strategies.

Although historically little attention had been given to domestic violence, even less effort had been devoted to address the hidden causes of abusive behavior. When looking at the causes of domestic violence and intervention methodologies to prevent it, two major social science perspectives emerge. These two perspectives have been the main focus for almost thirty years. One is a family violence perspective, and the other is the perspective from the paradigm of feminism. Family violence researchers view violence between husbands and wives (spousal abuse) as a pattern of violence occurring among all family members. Feminist researchers, in turn, place male/female relations at the core of their analysis. They view *inequality* between men and women as the key factor in domestic and family violence.

Causes of Domestic and Family Violence

Studies on causes of domestic violence help activists and researchers grapple with the complexity of real life. This complexity is a clear statement supporting the fact that domestic violence lacks refinement. The American Psychiatric Association (APA) task force chose domestic violence as part of a special theme in 1996. They found that the ability to collect accurate statistics has been hampered by the difficulty of identifying and defining what should be considered domestic violence.

Roles in Family Relationships

Roles in relationships have a magic-like power to alter how a person is being treated, how a person acts and feels; and what a person does and even thinks. This magic-like power applies not only to the developing person but to the others in the world. The relation in both directions of power struggle establishes the minimal and defining condition for the existence of a dyad, or twosome. Therefore, in any dyadic relation, and especially in the course of joint activity, what the one partner does influences the other and vice versa. Herein lies the balance of power, as roles are usually identified by the labels used to designate various social positions in a culture. These are typically differentiated by age, sex, kinship relation, occupation, or social status. Other factors such as religion and ethnicity may also come into play. Associated with every position in society are role expectations about how the holder of the position is to act and how others are to act in response.

An ethnographic study from ninety societies across the world identified four factors that when taken together are strong predictors in societies where violence against women is especially prevalent:

1. Economic inequality between men and women
2. A pattern of using physical violence for resolution of conflict
3. Male authority and decision-making in the family
4. Divorce restrictions for women

Further research indicates that female economic inequality is the stronger factor, strengthened by male control in the family and the wife's inability to divorce.

The Culture of Violence

A cross-cultural study suggests that rigid gender roles, especially concepts of masculinity linked to male dominance, toughness, or male honor are highly correlated with domestic or family violence. It was also found that violence against women is particularly prevalent in societies where the use of force as a means of resolving interpersonal conflict is condoned. The most violent husbands tended to make most of the decisions regarding family finances (Heise 1998). They also strictly controlled where and when their wives could go. Every child in the world is born into a particular culture, and from the moment of birth the custom into which he or she is born shapes his or her experience and behavior.

Factors such as poverty, racism, breakdown of the family, and inadequate societal support systems for working parents all play roles in domestic violence. These alone cannot account for the fact that the majority of persons arrested are men—as many as 90 percent. Females suffer from these conditions as much as males, yet they commit only a small portion of domestic violent crimes (Peled et al. 1995).

Masculinity

The major contributor to male violence is still a prevailing, obsolete factor of masculinity centered on toughness, dominance, extreme competitiveness, eagerness to fight, and repression of empathy. The socialization of boys has increasingly encouraged the concept of masculinity instead of moving away from it. The common approach that *boys will be boys* and that nothing can be done about it is but one example. The view by sociobiologists that males have developed a highly-aggressive killer instinct, and that the culprit is being perceived as being the hormone *testosterone,* is in no way being considered an inexorable instinct or drive by opposing researchers. Therefore, although men as a group have a potential for learning violent behavior, environment can make all the difference in terms of encouraging or discouraging such behavior.

The Role of Emotions in Domestic Violence

Emotions such as hostility and fear have been emphasized in literature relating to domestic violence. To gather first-hand data, researchers rely on reports by perpetrators and their victims, which are subjective, often biased and easily distorted. Jacobson and Gottman (1998) wanted to answer the question of whether emotions have practical implications for the lives of female victims. This could only be done through a controlled study. Their findings were that not all men who abuse their wives emotionally are batterers, but virtually all batterers also abuse their wives emotionally. They do so by verbal threats; intimidating actions, such as the destruction of pets or property; humiliating and degrading remarks; and robbing their partners of their autonomy as human beings. Once a woman has physically been battered, emotional abuse can be especially frightening and controlling.

Drug and Alcohol Abuse

Researchers found the most definitive role of alcohol use was one of the strongest indicators that men would be physically aggressive during their first year of marriage. It has also become clear that batterers are a great deal more likely to be substance abusers than are men who do not commit domestic violence. None of the research proved that alcohol or drugs caused violence; it simply suggests that violent men tend to have drug and alcohol problems (Jacobson and Gottman 1998). Substance abuse has been found to co-occur in as many as 60 percent of cases of domestic violence across various studies, and evidence suggests that substance abuse plays a facilitative role in intimate partner violence. Over 20 percent of males were drinking prior to their most recent and severe act of domestic violence. Research found that on days of heavy drug-use, physical violence was eleven times more likely. Thus, long-term substance abuse creates an environment that sets the stage for partner conflict and ultimately partner violence.

Anger

Voluntary behavior involves a choice. Depending on the outcome the person seeks, different choices will be made. Although some people suffer from temporal lobe epilepsy and uncontrollable impulsive behavior, the majority of batterers have a choice in the same sense that all other voluntary actions are choices. Therefore battering is usually voluntary.

A Closer Look at the Patriarchy

Historically, the *privilege* of beating one's wife has had social and legal approval in western civilization since ancient times. In 1824, wife beating was made legal in the state of Mississippi, United States. This, through court cases, resulted in reaffirming the traditional right of a man to beat his wife. During the 1870s, laws were passed that gave women meager protection against cruelty and allowed divorce on this ground. As most of the laws supporting a husbands right to physically punish his wife have been abandoned in the U.S., traditions of male entitlement and hierarchy lingers.

In this century at least, ideas such as the belief of personal privacy with the rejection of outside intervention of the family and the couple relationship also leave women to struggle alone against oppression. This is considered a good arrangement because it purportedly allows family members to be nurtured in an ambience of security and happiness. However, at the same time it appears to give protection from the outside world. The idea of peace, security, and harmony is still so strongly associated with the institution of the family that it has been very difficult to deal with the fact that many people are abused within the home environment. For many women and children, despite fears to the contrary, it is in the majority of cases not a stranger but a so-called loved one who is most likely to commit some sort of domestic violent action. Available statistics clearly show the high incidence of violence among family members, yet such information has usually been ignored, or given scant notice or treatment.

Etiology of Gender-Based Violence: An Ecological Framework

Although our understanding of the exact causes of gender violence lacks refinement, studies suggest that hierarchical gender relations, perpetuated through gender socialization and the socio-economic inequalities of society, are integrally related to violence against women. The ecological framework of gender-based violence may be described as consisting of four levels of analysis, best described as four concentric circles.

1. The innermost circle (core) represents the *personal history factors* that each person brings to a relationship. For men who are violent toward female partners, two developmental experiences have emerged as particularly predictive of future abuse: witnessing domestic violence as a child and experiencing physical or sexual abuse as a child. Having a rejecting or an absent father emerges as a possible predictor of future violence.

2. The next circle is the *microsystem,* which represents the immediate context in which intimate violence takes place. A variety of factors has shown to be related to the increased risk of sexual coercion, childhood sexual abuse and/or physical abuse of adult women. Factors referred to are the following:

a. Male dominance in the family;
b. Male control of wealth and finances in the family;
c. Marital conflict;
d. Use of alcohol and drug abuse.

3. The third level is the *exosystem*. It includes the institutions and social structures such as work, neighborhood, social networks, and other identity groups. In families with low incomes and unemployed men, violence is more common. Social isolation of women and family are both a cause and a consequence of wife-abuse. It had been reported that delinquent peer associations such as encouragement of sexual aggression play a major role. A culture of sexual access is also of paramount importance in the maintenance of self-esteem.

4. The fourth and last level is the *macrosystem*. This system generally views attitudes that make up the culture at large. On this level the emphasis is on the interrelationship of patriarchal beliefs and values. Factors such as the notion of masculinity linked to dominance, toughness, honor of men, rigid gender roles, and a sense of male entitlement over women are prominent.

Gender Inequality, Violence against Women, and Fear: A Feminist Perspective

The feminist theory holds the notion that violence against women results from gender inequality on the societal level, and the more unequally women are compared to men, the more likely men are to be violent against women. From this perspective, empirical test results show substantial support for the theory. The first main finding is that a structure of gender inequality is associated with a culture of violence. Also, that unequal educational and occupational status of women is correlated with the prevalence of sexual violence. Therefore, when women represent an equal balance in institutions of higher education or workplace, men may accept women as equal. Thus, men will not use forms of sexual violence. The second main finding is that sexual violence is associated with a culture of women's fear, and that a woman does not have to be a victim of violence to feel more fearful. The knowledge of violent acts is enough to instill fear in all women, regardless of personal experiences.

Psychology and Domestic Violence

Psychologists around the world believe that it is the interaction among gender, political structure, religious beliefs, attitudes toward violence in general, violence toward women, state-sponsored violence (civil conflicts and wars), and migration within and between countries that ultimately determine women's vulnerability and safety. State-sponsored wars often increase the amount of violence against women. Rape and brutal physical beatings have been considered the just spoils of war. Poverty, a direct result of war, is one of the major contributors to violence against women.

Resistance to change from law enforcement, judicial systems, health and social services, and organized religion, many of whom view the home as sacrosanct, all serve to condone, and in many cases facilitate, continued abuse in the family. Psychological research shows a strong relationship between violence in the home and violence in the community. Furthermore, psychological evidence clearly demonstrates that violence is learned behavior that is passed down from one generation to the next. The highest risk marker for a man to use violence against his wife or child is early exposure to violence in his childhood.

Child Abuse

Although disagreement exists on exactly what child abuse is, the tragedy of child abuse continues with signs of increase. The types of abuse can be physical, emotional, verbal, and sexual. It is the history of child abuse that led to the institution of Good Samaritan laws and practices in the U.S. It is also evident that most people agree that some kind of discipline is necessary. While public debate about related values and social issues escalates, many agree that controlled spanking is not the same as child abuse.

American statistics don't make for good reading. Thirty-five percent of runaway children leave home because of incest and 53 percent because of physical neglect. Some die from disease, exploitation, and malnutrition. Hoff (2001, 245) wrote "When dealing with individual cases of child abuse or neglect, especially if the parents were abused themselves or problems with alcohol are involved, it is easy to lose sight of the evidence that child abuse is rooted in the fabric of many societies." Economic hardships and stress are perfect breeding ground for unequal social opportunities. Childcare is perceived to be socially devalued in several practices in the United States. Further disturbing factors are that over three million children in the U.S. are at risk of witnessing violence between their caretakers with devastating consequences. Wars such as in Iraq, Afghanistan, Kosovo, Rwanda, and many others, like in Angola where I served in the South African Defense Force, have lasting devastation on children. They become traumatized. This type of trauma is something beyond comprehension.

SECTION TWO:
Intervention with Men Involved in
Domestic Violence

The Duluth Domestic Abuse Intervention Project: A Coordinated and Integrated Community Response

The full force of the criminal justice system is central to community-coordinated intervention. Experience in Duluth, Minnesota has shown that law enforcement and criminal justice systems can undermine some of the cultural support for domestic violence. The Duluth program enables the community to develop a more general strategy for decreasing all forms of violent behavior. The decision by the community to enforce assault laws and civil protection orders in domestic abuse cases has extensive impact on the law enforcement. This is also the case with the criminal justice systems of the community. The Duluth Domestic Abuse Intervention Project attempts to coordinate the program by protecting the victim:

1. It brings the perpetrator into the *criminal justice system.*
2. It enforces *legal sanctions* that will deter further acts of violence.
3. It provides safe *housing, education, and legal support* to the victim.
4. It serves as a tool to coordinate information flow and monitoring *procedures and policies.*

Community Activities and Roles

The Rural Domestic Violence and Child Victimization Enforcement Grant Program in Washington have identified outcomes associated with community enforcement success, which include the following:

- Monthly meetings comprised of community members
- Yearly community and school based presentation on violence prevention and intervention
- Distribution of posters with anti-violence messages
- Candlelight vigils for victims
- Prominent and consistent coverage of domestic violence in local newspapers
- An emergency 911 pager system for all

The emphasis is on the importance of community roles and the positive outcomes associated with it.

Changes in the Criminal Justice System

The major focus of community-coordinated interventions has been on changing the official criminal justice response through legislation and policy development. While many communities have forced police agencies to define guidelines for arrest practices, a Minneapolis experiment found that arrest produced the least repeat violence for the same victims.

Individual Safety Plan

In 1991, Roberts developed a seven-stage crisis intervention protocol. He promotes the idea that every individual in an abusive relationship should have a personalized safety plan. It provides a sequential framework for intervention on behalf of persons in acute psychological and situation crisis. This is necessary so that when victims of abuse make the decision to leave, they do it as safely and as expeditiously as possible.

Therapeutic Support

The lack of a single overall guiding therapeutic model, the ever ongoing search for the underlying principles, the growing acknowledgement that no one therapy is more correct than the other, leads to call for an integrated approach. Counselors are not limited to one therapeutic school. Many theories of therapy can be summarized by a few essential principles, or *processes of change*. In change, as in many other aspects in life, *timing* is paramount. The counselor will probably apply nine major processes: (1) consciousness raising, (2) social liberation, (3) emotional arousal, (4) self-evaluation, (5) commitment, (6) countering, (7) environment control, (8) rewards, and (9) helping relationships.

Further studies revealed that successful counselors used specific tools differently when the situation demanded a new approach. Specific time periods were reasonably constant from one person to the next. These periods were named *the stages of change,* which have six well-defined stages: (1) precontemplation, (2) contemplation, (3) preparation, (4) action, (5) maintenance, and (6) termination.

Facing the Facts

Gondolf and Russel's publication *Man to Man* (1987) was not to provide a secret formula or an instant cure for violence against women. They offered what other abusive men saw as lessons they have learned. They wanted to pass along some of their wisdom of experiences in their journeys as abusive men. Stopping abuse is to stop denying reality, stop blaming the woman, and face the facts. Abuse is just not worth it. Violence actually destroys the very ones we love and abusive men cause more harm than one realizes. When weighing the cost of abuse, the cost of a new direction can simply not be ignored. There are rewards in the end, and the first step in stopping abuse is to interrupt the cycle. It may mean separating from his partner for a while. It is also a way to let go of some of the control and to allow time for change (Gondolf et al. 1991).

The range of causes in domestic violence, the different levels within relevant disciplines, and the difficulty in defining it does not allow for a single intervention plan or technique. The variety of causes including internal personal psychological factors, gender inequality, general fear due to past violent experiences, etiology of gender, anger, patriarchy, drug and alcohol abuse, emotions, masculinity, gender roles in relationships, and cultural traditions demand interventions on all levels relating to such causes. A coordinated and integrated community response has a stake in intervention to curb domestic violence. What matters is the system in which it is embedded.

References

Bronfenbrenner, U. 1979. *The ecology of human development: Experiments by nature and design.* Massachusetts: Harvard University Press.

Ceasar, P. L., and L. K. Hamberger, eds. 1989. *Treating men who batter: Theory, practice and programs.* New York: Springer Publishing Company.

Dobash, R. E., and R. D. Dobash. 1980. *Violence against wives: A case against the patriarchy.* Somerset: Open Books Limited.

Dubnova, I. and D. M. Joss. 2000. Women and domestic violence: Global dimensions, health consequences and intervention strategies. *Work: A Journal of Prevention, Assessment, and Rehabilitation* 9.

Dutton, M. A., A. Warrel, D. Terrell, S. Denaro, and R. Thompson. 2002. *National Evaluation of Rural Domestic Violence and Child Victimization Enforcement Grant Program.* Final Report, Vol 1. Washington DC.

Easton, C. 2006. The role of substance abuse in intimate partner violence. *Psychiatric Times* 25(1).

Fals-Stewart, W., J. Golden, and G. R. Birchler, eds. 2003. Domestic violence. In *Handbook of behavioral treatments for psychological disorders.* Thousand Oaks: Sage Publications.

Feder, L., ed. 1999. *Women and domestic violence: An interdisciplinary approach.* New York: The Haworth Press, Inc.

Geffner, R., M. J. Barrett, and B. B. Rossman. 1995. Domestic violence and sexual abuse: multiple systems perspectives. In *Integrating family therapy: Handbook of family psychology and systems theory.* Washington. DC. APA Books

Gondolf, E. W., and D. M. Russel. 1991. *Man to man: A guide for men in abusive relationships.* Brandenton: Human Services Institute.

Heise, L. L. 1998. Violence against Women: An integrated, ecological framework. *Violence Against Women* 4(3).

Hoff, L. A. 2001. *People in crisis,* 5th ed. San Francisco: Jossy-Bass.

Jacobson, N. S., and J. M. Gottman. 1998. *When men batter women: New insights into ending abusive relationships.* New York: Simon and Schuster.

Kaufman, K. G., and M. Sraus. 1990. The drunken bum theory of wife-beating. In *physical violence in American families: Risk factors and adaptations to violence in 8,145 families.* Brunswick: Transaction Publishers.

Levinson, D. 1989. *Violence in cross-cultural perspectives.* Newbury Park: Sage Publications.

Peled, E., P. G. Jaffe, and J. L. Edleson, eds. 1995. *Ending the cycle of violence: Community responses to children of battered women.* London: Sage Publishers.

Prochaska, J. O., J. C. Norcross, and C. C. Diclemente. 1995 *Changing for good.* New York: First Avon Books Trade Printing.

Roberts, A. R., B. S. Roberts. 2005. *Ending intimate abuse: Practical guidance and survival strategies.* New York: Oxford University Press.

Sanday, P. R. 1981. The socio-cultural context of rape. *A Cross-Cultural Study Journal of Social Issues* 37(4).

Sherman, L. W. 1992. *Policing domestic violence: Experiments and dilemmas.* New York: The Free Press.

Tifft, L. L. 1993. *Battering of women: The failure of intervention and the case for prevention.* San Francisco: Westview Press.

Walker, L. E. 1999. Psychology and domestic violence around the world: Domestic Violence Institute and Nova Southeastern University. *American Psychologist Association* 54(1).

Yodanis, C. L. 2004. Gender inequality, violence against women, and fear. *Journal of Interpersonal Violence* 19(6).

Chapter Four

School Bullying

SECTION ONE:
Personal Violence in Schools

Personal violence in schools has a long and harrowing history. However, the systematic study of bullying only began in Scandinavia in the 1970s by Professor Dan Olweus. His studies were conducted in schools in Norway and Sweden, and his work focused on explanations as to why some children bullied and why some children were victimized. The outcome of the studies showed that children could be educated not to bully or be bullied.

When confronted with an issue of a child being bullied at school, it raises thoughts and questions whether the story is true. Is bullying possible or even real? Research into this phenomenon includes defining bullying in schools and determining the extent of bullying, the risk factors, consequences, and implications for counseling practice. As I did not personally experience bullying at school, I shall reflect my journey through counseling a little boy called Andrew.

The story of Andrew, a ten-year-old boy, is one that leaves little doubt that what he experienced left him scared, psychologically intimidated, and fearful. The fear became prominent when he was at school among certain classmates. For a period, when standing in lines, he was often pushed out of his position by another boy who was somewhat taller than Andrew. When Andrew tried to assert himself, he was threatened of being beaten-up to the point that he did not want to go to school anymore. From his perspective, Andrew believed that he was bullied and this, according to Rigby (2002), is only *one* approach in defining bullying *from the perspective of the child.*

Defining the Term Bullying

Bullying can be seen as a number of different forms of proactive aggression, depending on the motivation and the intention of the bully. In addition, they take the form of different kinds of systematic and aggressive social interactions. Bullying is also described as intentionally causing hurt to the victim and that this hurt can be both physical and psychological. Another definition sees bullying as physical or psychological violence by an individual or group against another who is not able to defend him or herself. It is a willful, conscious desire to hurt another and put him or her under stress.

The Scottish Council for Research in Education defines bullying is a willful, conscious desire to hurt, threaten, or frighten someone else. From this paradigm, one does not have to do anything. *Desire* is enough to make one a bully. For Rigby then, the question arises, "who is not a bully?" Furthermore, Rigby claims that the correlation between expressing the thought or desire to hurt someone else and then actually doing so is quite low for both boys and girls. As a definition, *the desire to hurt* is so broad that in practice it is actually useless.

Bullying versus Aggressive Behavior

It is evident that some researchers do differentiate between bullying and aggression, or at least interpersonal aggression, and as Rigby (2002) states, "it may seem like splitting hairs to make a distinction between aggression and bullying, but it is clear that some writers have been reluctant to use the term *bullying*, preferring the term *aggression*."

From Andrew's point of view it is clear that he experienced a degree of fear as he was often pushed around by a boy who was physically bigger and stronger than him. There seems to be a presence of aggression. However, has Andrew been bullied by this definition? This question takes us to a core element of power imbalance, which may arise from Andrew lacking enough power, strength, or will to assert himself when being pushed around. Bullying is essentially the abuse of power.

Extent of Bullying in Schools

Reports from around the world during the 1980s and 1990s suggested that bullying was prevalent in all schools. Contemporary studies in Australia have indicated that about one child in six or seven is being bullied, Smith et al. (1999, 327) write, "with quite unacceptable frequency." This refers to bullying on a weekly or more frequent basis. Further evidence suggests that there is significant increase in bullying when children move from primary to secondary school, and that age and gender are factors reported in bullying.

Cases since 1984 indicate that boys were more likely to be physical in bullying. Girls in contrast tended to be cruel verbally. Girls were also more often exposed to harassment such as slandering, spreading of rumors, and exclusion from a group rather than physical attacks. Although these differences are general, Olweus reminded researchers that in some cases girls were also physically bullied while boys do verbally attack one another. The first UK nationwide survey done on bullying by Kidscape in 1984 to 1986 revealed that 68 percent of children had been bullied at least once. Thirty-eight percent had been bullied at least twice. The concerning factor was that 0.5 percent of the children felt that it had affected their lives to the point that suicide was considered. They refused to go to school or ran away from home; some became chronically ill. Again, this is in line with Andrew's fear and why he wanted to rather stay home than go to school.

Risk Factors of Becoming a Bully or a Victim

The maturational or *taming process* has enabled the majority of people to end up as reasonably mature and caring citizens. Crime (bullying) in many cases was due to a failure in the taming process. Family background, genetic endowment, and cultural influences certainly affect the way a child will respond to others. This point of view is described by Geffner et al. (2001), saying that three risk factors fall firmly within the family circle:

1. A lack of parental warmth and involvement increases the risk that a child may become hostile and aggressive towards others.
2. Inappropriate aggression towards siblings and others, when permitted by parents, may lead to aggression towards others outside the family.
3. Children are more likely to be aggressive when parents use physical disciplinary measures.

Conoley and Goldstein (2004), write that families with aggressive children relate to five conditions that contribute to blaming between families and schools:

1. Social distance between families and schools
2. Family attitudes and beliefs about school environments
3. Quantity and quality of communication
4. Lack of clarity in the socialization roles
5. The nature of school policies and procedures

On one end of the scale, children who are bullied at home or who see their parents or siblings bullying may be more likely to be bullies in school. On the other end of the scale, children who lack close friends in school and who are often alone or who find it difficult to be assertive are more likely to be bullied. Those who are perceived as being different from the majority can also be at risk, such as children with special educational needs. These children were significantly more at risk of being bullied than mainstream children. Some two thirds of special needs children compared to a quarter of mainstream children with even a greater difference for children in secondary schools are at risk of being bullied.

The Consequences of Bullying in Schools

Consequences for bullies. In cases where bullying has been involved, legal action has been applied in relation to the nature of the assault and the damage it caused, rather than because it constituted bullying as such. From a legal point of view, it seems that bullying per se is not defined as a crime. Therefore only the actions accompanying bullying may seem to be criminal. They incur legally-justified punishment. In schools on the other hand, tribunals (courts) may be put in place to examine bullying with authority to sanction. Sanctions could include suspension of the child concerned. The buzzword has until recently been *consequence*, as this sounds better than punishment. The formulation of reasonable rules allows for the bullies to bring certain consequences onto themselves. This notion is echoed by Elliott (2002). He is of the opinion that whenever punishment is used, ethical considerations come into play in spite of the sufferings of the victim. Elliott further writes that if certain behavior is outlawed and is subsequently punished, there is a great likelihood that such behavior will in time be inhibited. Whichever way one looks at bullying in schools, it is important that there are consequences for this behavior.

Consequences for the victim. One of the most common effects on victims of bullying is the loss of self-esteem. This may lead to isolation. Research findings indicate that victims of bullying tend to have few friends, if any. Another result, when bullying is serious and sustained, is that a student may decide to avoid school, which in turn can lead to his or her academic work suffering. The general health of children who are victimized can be seriously affected. There is persuasive evidence of a link between suicide and other catastrophic health issues and bullying at school.

In many instances, responses to bullying invoke the idea of zero tolerance. There is the belief that allowing small crimes in a school or community to pass unpunished will encourage contempt for the law in larger matters. In practice, a school in which children tease and call each other names will also be one in which children physically assault one another. If, for instance, teasing is stopped, physical violence will be reduced.

Implications for Counseling Practice

School ethos. Research indicates that the incidence of bullying does vary from school to school. Although social, family, and personality factors do play an important role, the school ethos can create an environment that can be beneficial in dealing with bullying. The single most important thing a school can do to prevent bullying is have a clear policy to which staff, children, and parents are committed. If anything is going to change, the aim must be to influence the behavior and attitudes of all staff, children, and parents.

Community ethos. While schools with a caring ethos can positively contribute towards reduced bullying incidents, communities with a caring ethos can do the same. The support of all concerned people is needed to reduce harmful effects on the communal life of schools. In contrast to having a caring ethos, ignorance of school bullying can cause serious implications to counseling practice.

Bystanders. A child who witnesses bullying and chooses to be a spectator is another negative factor towards counseling. "Onlookers are part of the problem," say McCarthy et al. (1996). Thompson et al. (2002), suggest that peers were involved as collaborators or observers in about 90 percent of bullying episodes. Crime as a media story, the victim as a witness in a court case, revictimization, and the community perspective of *getting over it*, are all factors contributing towards counseling intervention.

My Personal Reflection on Researching Bullying in Schools

As I mentioned earlier, I did not experience any physical or any other major bullying during my school days. However, in researching of the topic I realized that if I had been to school in Australia I may have been one of six out of ten bullied. If I had been to school in the UK, I may have been one of four out of ten bullied. This reality had me at times thinking deeply of how easily an innocent child can become a victim of bullying, sometimes with harrowing effects.

Bullying in schools does not seem to be easy to define, as a variety of perspectives have been offered by writers and researchers. They do not ignore the fact that bullying is a reality and requires attention. There has been an evolution in the way in which bullying has been conceptualized, leading to ongoing improvements and refinements, which are being recognized. Rigby (2002), for instance, suggests that a distinction be made between malign and non-malign bullying—malign bullying being based upon analysis of published views of what bullying is.

> Bullying involves a desire to hurt + hurtful action + a power imbalance + repetition + and unjust use of power + evident enjoyment by the aggressor and generally a sense of being oppressed on the part of the victim.

Victims may be at greater risks for dysfunction after being bullied. Juvonen and Graham (2001) speculate that this could be, "because children differ in the way they (1) construe such events, (2) respond to aggressors or (3) manage, cope, or compensate for the feelings they experience during or after harassment." There are child factors that may moderate the potential impact by social domains and developmental psychopathology. Indications are that child characteristics may buffer or exacerbate the effects of stressors on children's adjustments.

Anxiety disorders may be one of the most prevalent disorders among children. In some cases, these disorders are co-morbid with other difficulties such as depression and conduct problems. While bullies report little anxiety, victims of bullying show higher rates of anxiety. The emotional and social problems associated with a history of being bullied are now well documented. Chronic victims of bullying are likely to view schools as unsafe places.

Research showed that the majority of children and parents were opposed to the secrecy in which some bullying issues were being dealt with. They perceived bullying as undesirable and believed that it should be stopped publicly. Olweus (1993) goes one step further in writing that one must also make use of sanctions; some form of negative consequences for undesirable behavior. I subscribe to this approach.

A Whole School Approach to Bullying

Having to deal with bullying, on the one hand, seems to be part of the daily function of the teacher. Yet, while I was researching the topic, and realizing the extent of bullying, I somehow compared it with the average manager in the workplace complaining that he cannot get his job done simply because he cannot get to it. The number of issues that lands on his desk that are unrelated to his primary task does not seem to go away. In a day fraught with demands on the teacher's time, handling an issue of bullying is just another one of a thousand things. I now have a better understanding of the extent and seriousness of bullying.

The *Whole-School* approach to bullying is a model that could reduce bullying in schools. Incorporating staff, parents, children, the greater community, and the local authorities in this initiative could all contribute towards a better outcome. A set of rules, policies, and procedures in handling bullying in schools; an understanding of the necessity of such; and the will to enforce them by all role-players would certainly have a positive impact. A combined approach of the school and the community will ensure that bullying is simply not tolerated in any way, shape, or form.

SECTION TWO:
The Bergen Anti-School Bullying Intervention Model

During the past decade we have seen considerable growth in community concern about bullying in schools. As a result, communities have required intervention strategies appropriate for addressing this problem. The anti-bullying intervention program against peer aggression within the school environment in the region of Bergen, Norway was considered a good model for other countries. It was adapted to the school settings of other countries.

Peer aggression and victimization within the school setting has, since the 1980s, been identified as a significant threat to the development of children and adolescent mental and social well-being. Observance revealed that the Bergen anti-bullying intervention research in the 1980s was the trigger for further research and action. It revealed that about one in seven students in Norway were involved with bullying or victimization. Supported by the National Ministry of Education, an intervention program employing a system-based approached was developed and disseminated in Norwegian schools aimed at reducing levels of peer aggression. From 1983 to 1985, some twenty-five hundred students (aged eleven to fourteen years) from forty-two schools in

Bergen were evaluated using a cohort-longitudinal study. Results showed a reduction of up to 50 percent in rates of bullying. The Olweus study was replicated in Rogaland, Norway, with seven thousand students aged between eight and sixteen years. It found slight increases in the amount of bullying. As differences in external support were observed, it was difficult to compare both evaluation studies. However, the positive results of the evaluation study in Bergen encouraged other countries to investigate the nature of the anti-bullying phenomenon in the school setting.

The Use of Model Programs

In a paper presented at *The Role of Schools in Crime Prevention Conference*, Rigby writes that numerous schools in Australia and overseas have developed and implemented anti-bullying programs. However, these have been with relatively limited attention paid to evaluating their successes. Furthermore, the comparisons made between recent results and social surveys of students from several years ago show no change in the incidence of reported bullying. This according to Rigby is a seriously flawed approach, as people during the 1980s thought of bullying as exclusively physical in nature. Today, they see bullying where they did not see it then.

Merely copying or replicating the model program could result in a concept that works in Bergen, Norway, but may affect other school settings in different ways. On the other hand, adaptation, which includes modification of the intervention to the new setting, may change critical aspects of the program. In turn, this could result in different interventions.

Intervention model programs can be described as evidence-based prevention programs. They are developed on an experimental or scientific basis, implemented on a large scale, and have to fulfill a set of quality criteria in a superior way. By comparing twenty-three intervention models in child and family mental health, Roberts and Hinton-Nelson (1996) identified six common characteristics of good model programs based on the following:

- Good theoretical foundation as to how the program is to improve the health conditions;
- A system-oriented approach;
- Recognizing both the individual and his or her environment;
- Intensive collaboration with multiple specialized services that reduces barriers to access for children and adolescents;
- Detailed information about program monitoring and outcome data;
- Criteria that allow good model programs to be replicated or adapted to other settings.

The Bergen anti-bullying program was inspirational to the adaptation processes of the Sheffield Bullying Project in England, the Anti-Bullying Intervention in Toronto schools in Canada, the Flemish anti-bullying project, the anti-bullying project of two towns in central and southern Italy, and the anti-bullying projects in Switzerland, Spain, and New South Wales, Australia.

Strengths of the Bergen Anti-Bullying Intervention Model

The primary aim of this model program is to increase adult and student awareness of problems of peer aggression and victimization. It endeavors to encourage active involvement of adults and peers in resolving bully-victim incidents. It aims to restructure the social environment by implementing clear rules and regulations. Additionally, these rules are meant to reduce the satisfaction bullies get while negative behavior becomes obvious. By stressing the reciprocal relationship between bullies or victims and their social environment, the program model can be defined as being founded upon a theoretical framework, inclusive of a need for a system-oriented approach. By encouraging network-forming links with school psychologists, social workers, counselors, parents, and teachers, barriers are being removed for children most at risk. Lastly, the program description provides an extensive report for evaluation.

How Successful is the Bergen Anti-Bullying Intervention Model Program?

Studies conducted between 1985 and 2001 shed some light on the effectiveness of anti-bullying programs. They reduced bullying among children between the ages of five and twelve years, and each of the studies involved measurements of bullying behavior at school before and after intervention. Subsequent studies found lower levels of self-esteem among children who reported being victimized.

Estimates were based upon self-reports of students as well as reports from teachers systematically observing children's behavior. Helen Cowie persuaded a number of teachers to employ so-called *cooperative teaching methods* in sixteen classes in two primary schools, having first assessed the number of bullying incidents. A small reduction in bullying was reported, though in general the researchers were disappointed with the outcome. However, of the nine programs using multiple procedures, eight evaluations provided clear evidence of a reduction in school bullying following the interventions. The largest was an average of a 50 percent reduction in reported school bullying in the Bergen area of Norway. For the most part the reductions were modest. An average reduction of 17 percent among primary school children was recorded. A final, but critical, observation was that reductions of school bullying were much greater in schools where the programs had been carried out most thoroughly.

Limitations of the Bergen Anti-Bullying Intervention Model Program

With regard to specific goals, methods, and monitoring procedures, some definite shortcomings were observed. The first observation was that the program appears unclear in indicating each target population. It did not specify what behavior and attitudes must be learned to fulfill the general program objectives of reducing the problems of bullying and victimization. No clear information was given about how program methods are linked to specific goals and lastly, what necessary skills were needed to conduct the intervention. In general, it was difficult to involve parents of bullies or victims in their home environment and this possibly limited the program outcomes. Notwithstanding the finding, teachers perceived the intervention as feasible and beneficial.

Characteristics of Adapted Intervention Programs

Systemic reviews of public health interventions should appraise the applicability of the intervention process. It should make provision for the adaptability of the intervention effectiveness to other localities. This should be based on knowledge of the intervention program and the new setting. While the impasse between the Bergen and the adapted program reflected such criteria, there are however adequate and solid models for program development. The intervention process model provides a plan for program development by sequentially combining theoretical findings, empirical information and data from target communities. It was therefore considered to be the most comprehensive model for program development. Activities within this stage are related to decision-making processes to either reject or to adopt an intervention that precedes the implementation phase.

Program Monitoring and Evaluation

The monitoring and evaluation stage was intended to carry out outcome evaluations directly related to the performance objectives. Pepler et al. (1994) noted that the adapted interventions were less effective in reducing bullying and victimization compared with the Bergen model. Also that less information was available on specific learning and environmental objectives, such as the increase in assertiveness of victims, self-control of bullies, child-rearing skills of parents, and teacher-student skills to interrupt bully-victim incidents.

Recommendations for Further Development

Although the findings were in favor of the Bergen model in that it fulfills most of the characteristics of *good* model programs, interested researchers suggested further development based on the following: First, programs need to formulate specific learning objectives, which were critical for focusing on the central attitudes, and behaviors of the *unhealthy* condition. Secondly, an overview of the learning objectives could provide a structure for more detailed evaluations. Lastly, program development in the various countries required clear guidance as well as regular monitoring.

What are the Implications?

The results were encouraging. Studies found that when intervention was started earlier rather than later, young children could be influenced to be less involved in bullying than older children. Therefore, early intervention is clearly very desirable. Additionally, evidence shows that intervention was more successful in helping all aged children to protect themselves from bullies than in stopping those who bully. Thus, intervention efforts need to become more effective in discouraging the behavior of those who bully others in school settings. Echoing Rigby's opinion is Sullivan (1999). He wrote that having an anti-bullying policy in schools is not enough; one must have effective practice. Parents and communities need to be part of the solution and not part of the problem.

The Bergen Anti-Bullying Intervention Model has shown positive outcomes in reducing rates of bullying behavior and victimization. The program has clearly indicated the essential components at each level of intervention and has provided reasons for program effectiveness. The catalyst for action in Australia to stop bullying in schools came from Europe. When few negative consequences result from parents, peers, or teachers from an aggressive act, bullying behavior will increase. Thus, anti-bullying intervention programs should restructure the social environment by implementing clear rules and regulations against bullying behavior. It was the work of Professor Dan Olweus that influenced the minds of those who were willing to eradicate bullying in schools.

References

Adamson, G., G. McAleavy, T. Donegan, and M. Shevlin.
2006. Teacher's perceptions of health ducation practice in
Northern Ireland: Reported differences between policy and
non-policy holding schools. *Health Promotion International.*
21(20).

Alsaker, F. D., and S.Valkanover. 2001. Early diagnosis and
prevention of victimization in kindergarten. In *Peer
Harassment in Schools* New York: Guilford Press.

Bartholomew, L. K., G. S. Parcel, and G. Kok. 1998.
Intervention mapping: A process for developing theory and
evidence-based health education programs. *Health Education
and Behavior* 25 (5): 545–563.

Conoley, G., and Goldskein, eds. 2004. *School violence
intervention: A practical handbook*, 2nd ed. New York: The
Guilford Press.

Elliott, M. 1991. *Bullying: A practical guide to coping for schools.*
Longman Group: U.K. ltd.

———. 2002 *Bullying: A practical guide to coping for schools,* 3rd
ed. Longman Group: U.K. ltd.

Geffner, R. A., M. Loring, and C. Young. 2001. *Bullying
behavior: Current issues, research and interventions.* New York:
The Haworth Press.

Genta, M. L., E. Menesini, A. Fonzi, A. Costabile, and P. K.
Smith. 1996. Bullies and victims in schools in central and
southern Italy. *European Journal of Psychology of Education.*

Juvonen, J., and S. Graham. 2001. *Peer harassment in school:
The plight of the vulnerable and victimized.* New York: The
Guilford Press.

McCarthy, P., M. Sheenan, and W. Wilkie. 1996. *Bullying: From backyard to boardroom.* Australia: Alken Press.

————, and S. Wilkie. 1998. *Bullying: A publication of the Beyond Association, Inc.* Nathan: QLD.

Olweus, D. 1992. *Bullying among school children: Intervention and prevention.* Newbury Park: Sage Publications.

————. 1993. *Bullying at School.* Oxford,UK.

————, S. Limber, and S. F. Mihalic. 1999. *Blueprints for violence prevention:* Book Nine; *Bullying Prevention Program.* Boulder: Center for the Study and Prevention of Violence.

Ortega, R., and M. J. Lera. 2000. *Aggressive behavior.* The Seville Anti-Bullying in School Project.

Pepler, D. J., W. M. Craig, S. Ziegler, and A. Charach. 1994. An evaluation of an anti-bullying intervention in Toronto schools. *Canadian Journal of Community Mental Health* 13.

Petersen, L., and K. Rigby. 1999. Countering bullying at an Australian secondary school. *Journal of Adolescence* 22.

Pitt, J., and P. K. Smith. 1995. *Preventing school bullying.* London: Home Office Police Research Group.

Rigby, K. 1996. *Bullying in schools: What to do about it.* Australia: Shannon Press.

————. 2002. *New perspectives of bullying.* Great Britain: Athenaeum Press.

————. 2002. *How successful are anti-bullying programs for schools?* Paper presented at the Role of Schools in Crime Prevention, 30 September–01 October 2002.

Rigby, K., and P. Slee. 1993. Dimentions of interpersonal relation among Australian children and implications for psychological well-being. *The Journal of Social Psychology* 133.

Roberts, M. C., and M. Hilton-Nelson. 1996. Models for service delivery in child and family mental health. In *Model programs in child and family mental health.* New Jersey: Lawrence Erlbaum Associates

Sharp, S., and P. Smith. 1994. *Tackling bullying in your schools: A practical handbook for teachers.* St Ives: Clays Ltd.

Smith, P. K., and S. Sharp. 1994. *School bullying: Insights and Perspectives.* London: Routledge.

———, Y. Morita, J. Junger-Tas, D. Olweus, R. Catalano, and P. Slee. 1999. *The nature of bullying: A cross-national perspective.* United Kingdom: TJ International Ltd.

———, and D. Thompson. 1991. *Practical approaches to bullying.* Exeter: BPCC Wheatons Ltd.

Stevens, V., I. De Bourdeaudhuij, and P. Van Oost. 2001. Anti-bullying interventions at school: aspects of program adaptation and critical issues for further program development. *Health Promotion International* 2.

Sullivan, K. 1999. Aotearoa/New Zealand. In *The nature of school bullying: A cross-national perspective.* New York: Routledge.

———. 2000. *The anti-bullying handbook.* New York: Oxford University Press.

Thompson, D., T. Arora, and S. Sharp. 2002. *Bullying: Effective strategies for long-term improvement.* Cornwell: TJ International Ltd.

Wang, S., J. R. Moss, and J. E. Hiller. 2005. Applicability and transferability of interventions in evidence-based public health. *Health Promotion International.* 21(1).

Chapter Five

Treatment for Anxiety and Post-Traumatic Stress Disorder

Recent studies reveal the surprising fact that anxiety disorders, not depression, were the most prevalent group of psychiatric diagnoses. This includes Post-Traumatic Stress Disorder (PTSD). Some 12.6 percent of adults in the United States over a period of one year were not diagnosed by mental-health professionals. They instead presented themselves in medical-care settings with PTSD-related physical complaints or for substance-abuse treatment. While the underlying anxiety frequently went unrecognized, patients complained about somatic symptoms such as heart racing, diarrhoea, chest tightness, dizziness, abdominal pain, and other anxiety related psychological and physical symptoms.

What is PTSD?

Often people suffering from PTSD have persistent, frightening thoughts and memories. They experience emotional numbness especially if their ordeal relates to people close to them. The event that triggers PTSD may be something that threatened the person's life or the life of someone close to them. Or it could be something witnessed, such as massive death and destruction after a building is bombed, a plane crash, or a serious car crash.

Whatever the source of the problem, some people with PTSD repeatedly relive the trauma in the form of thoughts and nightmares. They experience disturbing recollections of traumatic events. Hours or months following the event, people waver between the two main stages of PTSD: re-experiencing (also called intrusion) and avoidance of the event.

Often, *avoidance* or *denial* comes first, with *psychic numbing* dominating. People minimize the significance of the stress, forget it happened, feel detached from others, lose interest in life, daydream, and abuse drugs and alcohol. Janoff-Bulman (1989, 115) holds the notion that, "we attempt to incorporate the anomalous within the framework of existing schemas. And we persevere in retaining already existing schemas rather than developing new ones."

During the re-experiencing phase, people are on the edge and flooded by illusions, hallucinations, nightmares, and mental images. These are followed by sleeplessness, lack of concentration, and somatic anxiety. They relive the event, cannot think about anything else, and have a fear of going crazy.

There are three subtypes of PTSD (Maxmen and Ward 1995):

1. Acute form that lasts less than three months
2. Chronic form that lasts three months or more
3. Delayed-onset form which emerges at least six months after the traumatic event and has the worst prognosis

When people with PTSD encounter a circumstance similar to the original stressor they often re-experience the event as the stressor rekindles the symptoms. The degree and duration of symptoms are usually less severe if the trauma is caused by nature, such as a hurricane or hailstorm. They appear to be worse when the traumatic event was caused by people in cases such as rape and kidnapping.

When Does PTSD Start and How Long does it Last?

For most people PTSD starts within about three months of the event, while for some, signs of PTSD do not show up until years later. Many respond positively to treatment within six months, but records show that others may suffer from PTSD for longer periods.

The Causes of PTSD

PTSD fills people's lives with overwhelming anxiety and fear. It may be chronic, relentless, and can become progressively worse if not treated. It occurs after severe and traumatic incidents such as a fire, rape, mugging, military combat, tsunami, torture, kidnapping, child abuse, domestic violence, and holocaust. These events are considered more than *normal* bereavement:

- The person experienced, witnessed, or was confronted with death or serious injury of self or others
- The traumatic event is persistently re-experienced
- The person persistently avoids stimuli associated with the traumatic event
- The person experiences increased arousal of symptoms
- The disturbance causes clinical distress or impairment in the person's social and occupational life
- The person experiences any symptoms for more than one month

Other Common Features of PTSD

Physiological—Arousal Symptoms could include some, and in many cases all, of the following: racing heartbeat, fatigue/exhaustion, fast breathing, restlessness, excessive sweating, nausea, dizziness, and shaking or shivering.

Cognitive Symptoms may include perception of threat/visual images, poor concentration, intrusive thoughts, worrying, lack of control, and confusion.

Behavioral Symptoms by people suffering from PTSD can vary from avoidance of similar events or circumstances, to persistently seeking of reassurance, to total withdrawal from social interaction to isolation.

Can PTSD Happen To Anyone?

PTSD can happen to anyone, and it can happen at any time. While the most common cause in men is in military experience; in women, rape and sexual and physical abuse are the most dominant causes.

Men serving in the military most likely to get PTSD are younger, with less military training. There is also a presence of previous emotional or physical abuse, or previous psychiatric symptoms. Traumatic experiences that are more likely to cause chronic and severe PTSD relate to traumas involving witnessing the death of fellow soldiers and witnessing or participating in atrocities that endanger self and buddies.

Women who have been raped, on the other hand, are more likely to develop PTSD if physical force, display of a weapon, or injury occurred. They tend to have more guilt, shame, and suicidal ideation.

PTSD can occur at any age, but elderly people and children experience more difficulties in coping with traumatic events.

Differential Diagnosis

In many instances PTSD goes undiagnosed for the following reasons:

- People do not report their traumatic experiences or subsequent symptoms
- Symptoms are easily masked by substance abuse
- Traumatic visual imagery is misattributed to schizophrenia

Also aligned with the difficulty of diagnosing PTSD is the tendency to use this illness to justify financial compensation. The person may not be able to distinguish reality from fabrication. They may represent their own version, rather than that of PTSD. Careful observation and coaching could help to get the correct diagnosis.

Anxiety disorders, major depression, compensation neurosis and adjustment disorder include the differential diagnosis. It is important to note that adjustment disorder with anxiety should not be confused with PTSD.

Treatment

Early treatment relating to traumatic experiences has its advantages. Debriefing immediately after the trauma can reduce the victim's chances of developing PTSD. A typical debriefing session of two hours incorporates four phases: (1) disclosure of events, (2) exploring the traumatic reactions, (3) identifying practical coping strategies, and (4) exploring any feelings of the disaster, action-plan transition, and attempts to leave the disaster.

Often victims of traumatic events will only accept support from people who have experienced similar situations. This is based on the misbelief that only such people will understand and emphasize with them.

Can Psychodynamic Therapy Help?

Psychodynamic therapy is helpful in that previous adaptive defenses are removed. Traumatic memories and reminders are gradually explored to create a safe therapeutic environment. The counselor can help the client to gain insight and understanding around the reasons for the problems. In therapy, the emphasis is on the counselor's ability to use what happens in the immediate to explore the types of feelings and dilemmas that have caused difficulties for the client.

The method used in psychodynamic therapy is called "free association." While the client is lying in a relaxed position, he or she can say whatever comes to mind. The stream-of-consciousness material that emerges from this procedure often includes strong emotions, deeply buried memories, and childhood experiences of traumatic events.

Can Cognitive-Behavioral Therapy (CBT) Help?

In CBT exposure approaches are used to reduce fear responses to both the original traumatic experiences and present mental reminders. CBT further focuses on distorted views of basic life assumptions regarding self-invulnerability, life meaningfulness, equitability, and positive self-esteem. The counselor can focus on the factors that maintain the client's anxiety by exploring situations the client is avoiding due to the event, places, people, noises, and alcohol or drug use and by interpreting life-threatening symptoms and thinking patterns that involve catastrophic, all-or-nothing, over-generalization type automatic thoughts.

In exploring the above the counselor will get a good sense of the person's anxiety levels. It can be determined whether they are generalized or situation specific, how they may have developed and how they are being maintained.

Do Support Groups Have Any Role to Play?

Well-established and effective support groups can help. They can provide practical support to the person's reactions of traumatic events by reinforcing it as *normal.* This is done while attending to common fears, concerns and traumatic memories. Support by an established and effective group can increase the person's ability to handle disturbing emotions while sharing strategies for coping with the situation.

Is Medication an Effective Treatment?

Medication can be used adjunctively with therapy for some symptoms of PTSD. Notice should be taken that there are a variety of medicines available, such as phenelzine, imipramine, anticonvulsant carbamazepine, adrenergic blockers, and benzodiazepines, for different types of responses. For more specific detail consult Maxmen and Ward (1995).

Self-Help Advice to Persons with PTSD (National Institute for Mental Health 2005)

- Acknowledge distressing experiences and reactions to it.
- Reinforce that these reactions are not abnormal.
- Avoid overuse of alcohol or other drugs.
- Avoid making major life-changing decisions.
- Do not bottle-up feelings, rather talk to someone you trust.
- Endeavor to keep to a normal routine.
- Do not avoid social activities and places unnecessarily.
- When fatigue creeps in, allow for enough rest.
- Let family and friends know of your situation.
- Deal with memories and reminders of events separately.

Researchers have in the past decade learned much about PTSD. New technology such as brain scan images and gene tests have brought new light to PTSD and related impairments. Although progress has been made there is still much more to explore, and hopefully new and revised treatment models will bring relief to those people suffering from this dreadful illness.

References

Graham, H. L. 2004. *Cognitive behavioral integrated treatment.* West Sussex: John Wiley and Sons, Ltd.

Janoff-Bulman, R. 1989. Assumptive worlds and the stress of traumatic events: Application of the schema construct. *Social Cognition* 7(2).

Johnson, D. W., and F. P. Johnson, 2003. *Joining together,* 8th ed. Boston: Pearson Education.

Maxmen, J. S., and N. G. Ward. 1995. *Essential psychopathology and its treatment,* 2nd ed. New York: W. W. Norton and Company.

McLeod, J. 2003. *An introduction to counseling.* Maidenhead: Open University Press.

National Institute of Mental Health. 2005. http://www.nimh. nih.gov/topics/ptsd.shtml

Chapter Six

Loss and Grief

SECTION ONE:
Reflections on My Personal Journal

The following reflections from my personal journal will incorporate criteria of loss that have specific meaning to me. The selected reflections represent my thoughts, feelings, and understanding of the concept of loss. This does not imply that other factors did not have significant value or impact on my thinking. Instead, they form a critical part of what I had experienced and have contributed to my better understanding of the concept of loss and grief.

Building a Framework of Loss

Schools of thought regarding loss such as the non-linear, chaos theory, circular grieving, humanistic, and transpersonal models are concepts and theories building on the framework of loss. An extension of this is that of respect, understanding, and enablement, which is contextual enough to bring understanding of the person's story. An integrative model is better demonstrated through specifically developed questions that systematically come to understand the story of loss. Integrative models contain some elements of different theories and may be divided into five main areas:

1. The world that was before the person experienced loss
2. The world the person is currently experiencing after the loss
3. The person's current profile
4. The road to healing
5. Those issues that prevent the person from healing

In short, these five areas are based on the specific questions as posed by the counselor at the time of counseling. They will contribute significantly to the counseling practice and will provide the counselor with a systematic framework for data collection that can be used in a consistent manner.

Growth and Deterioration

As the experience of loss becomes integrated into the basic psychological function of a person, there exists the potential for either personal growth or deterioration. From this perspective, the psychological outcome can contribute to personal capacity building and lead to positive change in relationships, philosophy, and priorities. Comments such as "I am a better person," "I have learned from this," "I appreciate life more," and "Life gives me better meaning," are common among people who have experienced loss of some significant sort.

At the same time, loss can also cause an extreme deterioration in life that may have the opposite outcome. Stereotype statements like *suffering is good* and *time will heal* need re-evaluation by those who inconsiderately use them. A third dimension is that both positives and negatives may be needed in the healing process. Research in this area shows that the *full story* of loss is required to identify growth elements. It is important to understand the context of the loss experience as well as the person. It will enable healing to manifest itself in the counseling process.

Traumatic Events: The Impact on People

When one looks at traumatic events and the impact that they have on people it comes as no surprise that people's responses vary from little change in behavior to severe and radical change. It can also have a ripple effect on others. Traumatic experiences are in many instances ignored as we do not think of the ripple affect they may have. Sometimes we simply fail to connect the events to the wider ring of circumstances. A lack of understanding of the repercussions may lead to unaddressed and hurtful situations. To demonstrate the impact of trauma and the ripple effect that it has can be described in a case of a single motor vehicle accident. What about the loved ones of those killed, the injured, those involved but not injured, family and friends, community, emergency services staff, and connected people?

In many cases trauma can lead to life-changing circumstances as well as peri-traumatic responses. Peri-traumatic responses are ways that the person naturally responds to avoid the trauma. It may lead to dissonance, avoidance, multi-personality disorders, preemptive strike (violence), anger, and depression. In many instances it leads to drug abuse, alcoholism, and abnormal sexual behavior. When people are unable to control their actions, the psychic apparatus will automatically perform the necessary action that will play out in peri-traumatic responses. It is important to acknowledge and understand the impact of a traumatic experience and the ripple effect that it has on people connected to the traumatized person.

Understanding the impact that traumatic experiences have on individuals is not an easy and simple concept to deal with. Identifying the differences between Acute Stress Disorder (ASD) and Post-Traumatic Stress Disorder (PTSD) is essential. It could determine a different way to the counseling process of healing. Some people experience a cluster of symptoms, which add to the importance of knowing and understanding the different classifications associated with trauma and grief. The emergence of a third category namely *traumatic grief* is being debated.

Trauma Continuing

Some losses do not have easy to identify symptoms. At times it becomes quite difficult to connect symptoms and behaviors to a specific event. In such cases the symptoms and behavior prolongs for a long time and can periodically play out in episodes surfacing as the person is unable to put the issue in the back of the mind. This type of loss is known as *chronic sorrow.* Some examples of chronic sorrow include unsolved murders, infertility, and degenerative diseases.

In many of these instances people experience the feeling of being trapped or humiliated. This is one of the worst mental situations to be caught up in. Feeling trapped seems more prevalent in cases of chronic sorrow. It is very useful to know how to address people suffering from chronic sorrow. The best method for these cases is first to inform the person or family that their experiences are not crazy. Secondly, it is paramount to help them understand their position on a specific day or time. Lastly, the counselor can introduce the using of identifiable objects to communicate their respective feelings and situations (a client of mine used a red armband when she felt extremely irritable and angry).

Loss is an integral part of trauma. There are differences between certain types of trauma, such as the difference between chronic sorrow and bereavement grief; chronic sorrow and prolonged grief; and chronic sorrow and depression. It is not only important to understand such differences but also to understand that loss threatens our assumptions about the safety of our personal worlds. The two main questions about safety are: how do the clients define being safe or unsafe; and how do they define authentic safety? Also important are the three levels of safety:

- Internal—that is, our emotions, thoughts, feelings and reasoning
- Interactional—our ways of communication and other social skills
- Organizational—the policies, practices and structures pertaining to mental health systems

Respect, Understanding, and Enablement

Each person has their own internal view of giving meaning to the experiences of loss and their way of grieving. Some individuals live their respective lives securing their privacy. Others may see the same things in a different way, therefore there exist different ways of coping with loss.

People have different internal capacities to cope with loss. External factors such as social support, and how the world perceives loss, play a major role in giving meaning to loss experience. They also have their roles in the healing process. From a holistic perspective, loss threatens our safety, our internal feelings of security, our own mastery, and in many cases our own control of our life. Yet personal experience of loss may create self-knowledge that is a gift to understanding ourselves and others. The value of self-knowledge, social support, and the understanding of coping mechanisms are crucial elements to the healing process.

SECTION TWO:
Case Example: Ann

This case study is primarily concerned with the study on Ann in her experience regarding the death and loss of her father. It is constructed in a format that will refer to her experience of losing her father through death. Ann's experience exemplifies theories relating to the subject of loss and grief in counseling. It departs from the paradigm (Raphael et al. 2001) that grief is not a disease.

Ann was a sixty-year-old Australian single lady. She held a corporate position where she had been for some thirteen years. At the time of our first meeting, Ann was dealing with a significant loss.

As a single person, she was very close to her father and respected him greatly. His maturity and wisdom stood out to her as he played a very prominent role in her life. She often used his advice when she had to make important decisions. She still remembered the time when she resigned from her former employer prior to take up her new position. To resign was a decision she made without any input from her father. This was a major issue in her life and she expected some repercussions in response from her father. However, she was very surprised to find that he was happy about *her* decision.

After her father's death, Ann experienced her father's presence in the house at times. She said that this feeling got stronger during evenings when she was alone in the house. This experience had lead to many sleepless nights. The good times they spent together from her childhood days until a few days before he died were still fresh in her mind. She also remembered those things that a responsible father had to share with her when she was out of line. She had kept a few items that belonged to him such as a shirt, some photos, and furniture; she felt that it helped her not to be alone. It helped her to refresh her memories in the ways that she remembered him despite the fact that she had rearranged the furniture and other interior items. She also bought a new car and was due to collect it on the day of our first interview.

Her uncle, who was seventy-four-years-old and was a retired medical doctor, had been visiting her more regularly since the death of her father. Although Ann had a good relationship with her uncle in the past, this relationship had grown stronger in the days since her father's death. In the absence of her father, she made use of her uncle's advice in making decisions of importance.

She had lost a great friend and companion as well as someone who shared a lot of wisdom in their relationship. This mature attitude was the core element for their close relationship. It allowed for social interaction as well as a relationship of trust. He was a person Ann could rely on, especially when she needed someone that could secure her environment. Then, more often her life felt empty and lonely.

Our first meeting was focused around her feeling lonely and guilty, with fluctuating swings of sadness. The feeling of her father's presence that Ann had during evenings when she was alone could have been a psychological response to the loss due to her close and precious relationship that she had with him. The thought that he had only been gone for a short period of three to four weeks was still very raw and active. The sense of his presence is viewed as a cognitive response, or even a degree of hallucination. Recent research in *thanatology* within the study of attachment theory has found that infants, as well as adults, develop relatively stable relationships. Loss through death has vast implications in the understanding of grief and mourning. Thus, people with particular attachment patterns will be more vulnerable to specific grief-related difficulties, while those with an avoidant style may experience the absence of grief. The idea that Ann would have responded overwhelmingly with emotions in her experience if she had an insecure attached relationship with her father. At first there did not appear to be any of these emotions present.

When Ann's experience of her father's presence was evaluated from the paradigm of *melancholia*, it did not fit the picture. From this perspective her experience would be considered *a refusal to let go*. There were no concrete signs of this behavior. However, she had to come face to face with the fact that he was gone and would not return. Ann did not show any abnormal grieving behavior, her emotions seemed moderate. She appeared healthy and reported to have been eating well. Stroebe (2002) describes these symptoms as being normal and therefore she is grieving for a loss of someone with whom she had a healthy and secure relationship.

Ann showed that she also had time and energy to put into her very responsible work. She was only absent from work for three days for the arrangements and attendance of the funeral. Although it was somewhat early in the process, Ann was adapting to a major loss by plowing energy into her work and daily life.

Human coping resources play a critical role in adjusting emotional responses to stressful experiences, which include interpersonal loss. These coping resources are referred to as an ability of the human emotion to protect the person from the destabilizing nature of a significant loss. Other traits such as conscientiousness, agreeableness, and perceived confidence also act as buffers in the effort to cope with the situation of grief.

Another symptom and physical response was Ann's loss of sleep. Apart from sleeplessness she had not shown any other physical responses or made any negative comments to this regard. She had already consulted her family doctor and had responded well to medication. During discussions Ann displayed openness, and she expressed that she was not aware of repressing any other emotional or physical experiences. The implications of repressing sorrow or other emotional expressions could lead to serious physical disorders and an impaired immune system.

Ann had decided to keep a shirt of her father's, one that she bought for him and had a special connection to. He used to wear it around the house when he did some light maintenance work and when he was engaged with his hobbies. As a linking object it brought comfort in her life, and it was also helpful as a conscious strategy when she needed to make decisions that would cherish her circumstances. This also related to the other belongings that she had kept. However, she did not seem to be preoccupied with these items.

Ann always depended on her father's advice, and now that he was not there, this role was being replaced by her uncle. Her uncle was a retired medical doctor and was helping her make decisions. At her initiative, he was also being a friend with whom she could socialize. In doing this she was in some way maintaining a secure bond with her father. As Servaty-Seib (2004) describes it, "Healthy recovery in the face of mourning, in the attachment perspective, entails finding a way to maintain a secure bond with the attachment figure while simultaneously acknowledging that the person is not physically available to provide comfort and care."

Accepting her uncle in a closer relationship after her father died could be noted as important and normal. Ann retained a secure and safe environment to continue her life without her father. Her uncle's role in supporting Ann in making important decisions had value in her surviving in the absence of her father. It allowed Ann to continue with her life in a way and manner, although not the same as with her father, that gave her stability when confronted with hard decisions. The aim of early and adult life attachment behavior is to enable continuation in bonds that are affectionate and acceptable. Not only had she accepted this closer relationship with her uncle to support her in making important decisions, but also to establish a closer relationship to fill her life in the domain of social activity.

Ann mentioned how her uncle had visited her more often. She naturally responded to her experience and emptiness by letting her uncle into a private part of her life. Ann was one of many people who, through heart sore and bitter experience, have come to know the process of grieving.

The memories that Ann had of her father were of good things that go back as far as childhood. But none were regretful and nor did she carry any guilt with them. The *self* is greatly influenced by losses and simultaneously the *self* is also influenced by people's efforts to process them. Therefore we cannot separate the self from memories. Should these memories be troublesome and not being dealt with, they will lie dormant in the mind and periodically be triggered by experiences during daily life. As our relationships with others provide a storage place for our shared memories, the loss of relationships undermine our stories and with it our identities.

Looking back at the mourning process that Ann had gone through and the grief that she had experienced regarding the loss of her father, it became clear that the major loss in her life was firstly, her father as lifelong friend, and secondly, her father as decision maker and advisor. However, there were secondary losses pertaining to her relationship in a social context and the environment of her profession.

Ann seemed to find herself in the very early stage of mourning as she was still very close to her father, so much so that his presence was often experienced as a reality. Making meaning of her experience was for her to find a balance between herself and how she engaged in the world around her, i.e., developing a meaningful life in the absence of her father. Ann benefited from counseling and support in helping her to progress through these stages.

Whether grieving is *normal* or *chronic* is difficult to say. *Normal* grief is seen as a reaction to loss, followed by a gradual return to normal life. On the other hand, *chronic* grief is a maladaptive reaction followed by a manifestation of psychological and physical impairments.

The symptoms of intrusive thoughts and feelings of loss, the yearning and searching for the absent figure and numbness about the loss are associated with complicated grief (CG). CG usually includes negative attitudes and unwillingness to accept loss, but these did not seem to be present in Ann's case.

Buying a new car and rearranging the house and furniture in a way that then suited her lifestyle, was seen as typical responses to moving on. However, it was in contrast with her experiencing her father's presence in and around the house. This behavior fits within the theory of the *Dual Process Model of Coping with Bereavement* where stressors, as well as the oscillation between the two stressors, are essential for adaptive coping. The most important aspects necessary to reconcile the mourning process are the desire to stay connected and the need to move on.

The first task of mourning is to recognize and accept the loss. The other three tasks are the following:

- Experiencing and working through the feelings related to grief;
- Reorganizing into a new and changed life;
- Emotionally relocating the deceased and moving on with the newly reorganized life.

Of importance is that individuals do not necessarily go through these stages in sequence but may complete them in different sequences.

Also applicable was the "person-centered" therapeutic relationship as Ann was involved in a relationship with her father where his death denied her to continue with this relationship. In a therapeutic counseling relationship, *necessary and sufficient conditions* needed to be present to have brought about change in her behavior. While empathy and other supportive characteristics such as consistency, boundary awareness, and interpersonal sensitivity played a crucial role, Ann was to be encouraged to accept and act on her own personal internal evaluations.

Had Ann continued experiencing the presence of her father in a way that was emotionally overwhelming to her and with feelings that would have lead to maladaptive and degradable life, she would have benefited from therapeutic intervention and treatment through Gestalt counseling. Ann had shown that she was moving towards self-regulation in many ways, however she was still struggling with the connection to her father as if he was still alive. The main technique is the reflecting of feelings in a non-directive way and selection of the most threatening stressor. When this most pressing stressor is addressed, the life figure she had of him in her mind would have moved into the background and the next stressor would have taken its place.

Another method of intervention is emphasized within the epistemology of cognitive-behavioral therapy (CBT). The primary emphasis of connecting meaning of loss (confronting Ann with issues relating to her personal responsibility) is useful in narrative orientations. She could tell and re-tell her story in counseling and in doing so, she could have established new and fresh perspectives through reassessing and reorganizing the patterns of her life. Furthermore, through rational-emotive therapy (RET) and transactional analysis (TA), Ann could have been guided to think in a rational way: "It is not the event itself but how the client thinks about the event that is the problem" (Barbato and Irwin 1992). The counseling relationship demands professionalism towards clients while it simultaneously leans towards flexibility, acceptance, and balance for both the counselor, and in this case, Ann.

As reflected in the above case, a number of theories relating to mourning and grief have cautiously been evaluated and integrated to address Ann's situation. Some correspond directly to her circumstances while others are either difficult to marry up or have no relation to this case in any way. The dual model process, attachment theory (meaning reconstruction of loss), the four stages of mourning, and the person-centered approach all offered direction in supporting Ann.

SECTION THREE:
Body Dysmorphic Disorder: An Area of Loss

As a practicing counselor I have found it useful to have a set of guide lines at hand with the most up-to-date and well-researched information. As it is difficult to find an up-to-date set of guide lines for BDD, I decided to compile this one. It reflects the latest information available in the area of Body Dysmorphic Disorder (BDD). It focuses on the impact BDD has on people experiencing loss. It is written in a format that is easy to use while it presents an overview of the area of loss. It also provides information that will help to identify problems that may occur as well as options available for caring for those people affected by a loss due to BDD.

A Historical Perspective and General Overview

Historically, BDD, or bad self-image, was referred to as *dysmorphophobia* or *beauty hypochondria*. The word dysmorphic comes from the Greek and means *ugliness of face*. BDD was classified as a particular disorder in acknowledging the extreme disparagement that some people experience regarding some aspect of the body and the physical appearance thereof. The American Psychiatric Association (APA) has BDD contained in qualifying criteria. It states that the disparagement should not be of delusional intensity and that "individuals should be able to acknowledge that their concern is excessive." The latter is in my mind a matter for debate.

Studies have found that 93 percent of women and 82 percent of men care about their physical appearance and try to improve it. The daily lives of people are filled with thoughts and wishes as to how they can change their appearance such as being taller, thinner, having a smoother skin, enlarging their breasts, or having a flatter stomach. Studies by World Vision (reported in a news bulletin by the Australian Broadcasting Corporation) among young people the past six years have shown that Australian young people are most concerned about their physical appearances—especially their weight. They will go to great lengths to changed their appearance. Multiple surgeries and body modification efforts such as compulsive weightlifting have, in some cases, failed to change their view. The primary distinguishing characteristic of BDD is not only a dislike of a perceived defect of a part of the body but an obsessive preoccupation with it. The question is: when does a concern become an obsession?

The *Wolf Man,* Freud's—and also one of psychiatry's—most famous patients may have suffered from BDD. No symptoms were documented by Freud; however, Ruth Brunswick, the second psychoanalyst who treated the Wolf Man in 1928 noted that he "neglected his daily life and work because he was engrossed, to the exclusion of all else, in the state of his nose; his life was centered on the little mirror in his pocket" (Clausen, 2005).

Etcoff (1999) notes the interest in beauty throughout history and claims that there exists cross-cultural consistency in the perception of attractive facial features. This phenomenon relates to men as well as women. Etcoff goes on to observe that a variety of species attend to exaggerate displays, such as the large and colorful tails of the peacock and the large antlers of the reindeer. Humans also prefer the exceptional, tempting men to over exercise their biceps and pectoral muscles, women to undergo breast implants and starve to retain a 0.70 waist-to-hip ratio, and voters to elect the taller candidate.

Features and Characteristics of BDD

BDD is described as an internal view of one's own appearance—how we see ourselves. It is multifaceted with the issue of accuracy of one's body perception as opposed to how other people see us. It consists of subjective measurements, over- or under-estimation of bodylines, such as the form or size of the nose, the size of the mouth, and the amount of facial hair. However, "more often the perception is not truly distorted; but rather, some aspect of appearance is disliked, disparaged, or seen as unacceptable."

Our internal subjective measurements may indicate high levels of dissatisfaction, negative thoughts, or cognitions associated with certain body sites. They may indicate high levels of social avoidance and may lead to high levels of occupational dysfunction. At the same time, elevated levels of depression and anxiety may occur in individuals. All these indicators may be due to negative feelings about the body or parts of the body. It is very difficult, if not impossible, to see a person's body the way that they see it. Obsessions related to BDD can manifest as excessive disproportionate concerns about a minor body defect or it can manifest as recurrent thoughts provoking anxiety about an imaginary defect.

Studies have found that men and women tend to obsess over different areas of the body. For this reason, men are more likely to stay unmarried. Furthermore, women are more likely to receive non-psychiatric medical and surgical treatment. The most common imaginary defects are of the face and include freckles, acne, the size and shape of the nose, size and form of the mouth, size and form of the ears, excessive facial hair, and the shape of the chin. Other parts of the body that would be more rarely complained about are the feet, hands, breasts, genitals, and muscles.

Areas such as hair, eyes, thighs, abdomen, chest size, shape, lips, scars, height, and teeth are also included. According to Clausen (2005), research has identified differences in the most common areas of obsession between men and women:

- **Men.** Hair (thinning or excessive body hair), height, chest, and genitals
- **Women.** Breasts, legs, and continuous checking in the mirror

Causes of BDD

There is little definitive research on the causes and etiological factors of BDD that predispose an individual. A great portion of the work comes from examining case studies and the information that people relate to the onset of symptoms. In many instances a single negative comment or a simple tease directed at the physical appearance of a person could trigger an initial focus on a specific body part.

An in-depth interview may bring to surface information that could help in making a correct diagnosis. Measuring an individual's behavioral responses to appearance-related situations provides useful data. The use of a questionnaire with a listing of body parts for anxiety ratings is usually of value. Marks and Mishan (1988) describes the avoidant behavior of a twenty-one-year-old female who believed that people laughed at her facial hair, body, and legs. She had reached the point where she covered her face with a scarf and motorcycle helmet. She also dressed and undressed in the dark to avoid her self-perception of her face and hair. Another female who believed that her cheeks and lips were too red repeatedly did mirror checking. She avoided food that would moisten and highlight the red color of her cheeks and lips.

Compulsive Behaviors by People with BDD

Most people with BDD engage in compulsive behavior in the hope that such behavior will make them look different. There is also the belief that they will feel worse if they do not behave in a certain way. Studies have shown that some four-fifths of people with BDD will spend many hours gazing in the mirror in the search to know exactly how they look, only to find that they feel worse after mirror gazing. Depression and suicidal behavior are not uncommon, and BDD may lead to extreme avoidance behaviors such as isolation from loved ones.

Apart from excessive mirror-gazing there are many other compulsive behaviors. Camouflaging of body parts with flattening clothes, excessive grooming, and overly-done makeup are more common. Some repetitively ask for reassurance about their looks and engage in frequent medical visits (especially to dermatologists) and multiple medical procedures such as plastic surgery.

Prevalence of BDD

No known research studies on the prevalence of BDD have been conducted. Between 1 and 2 percent of the general population and some 15 percent of psychiatric outpatients have been affected. There is a belief among some researchers that prevalence is on the rise as diagnostic methods become more advanced. In contrast to eating disorders where some 90 percent of cases are females, studies suggest that BDD may be equally common in adult males and females. Among adolescents, only 9 percent were found to be boys.

Co-Morbidity with Other Psychological Disorders

BDD and Anorexia Nervosa. There seems to be a relationship between BDD and other psychiatric disorders such as obsessive-compulsive disorder (OCD) and anorexia nervosa. Someone with an eating disorder may show symptoms of body dysmorphia especially in cases where there are signs of body image disparagement for a weight-related body site such as waist, hips, or thighs. When BDD is related to a non-weight-related site (nose, mouth) the indications are that there is no co-occurring eating disorder. Importantly, if the BDD site of interest is a weight-related site, assessment should be focused on usual eating disordered symptoms of excessive dieting, weight loss, purging, and feelings of loss of control regarding food.

The similarities between BDD and anorexia nervosa are often hidden. The person with BDD is preoccupied with the appearance of the body with repetitive body measuring and mirror gazing. Anorexia nervosa, on the other hand, is a disturbance of the whole body. It affects more women than men, and the age of onset is typically sixteen years old, as opposed to twenty years. Finally, BDD more commonly involves rituals such as mirror-gazing and brushing hair, etc.

BDD and OCD. The relationship between BDD and OCD is more difficult to determine. Some researchers and clinicians are of the belief that BDD is an OCD spectrum disorder; i.e., the core symptoms are the same but in the case of BDD the focus is on body appearance.

Similarities between BDD and OCD are, as in the case of

anorexia nervosa, often secret. It consists of obsessional thoughts that are difficult to resist or control. They are both debilitating disorders featured by doubting, worry, and anxiety.

The differences between BDD and OCD are firstly that BDD focuses on defective body appearance. OCD often involves fears such as becoming ill, causing harm, and the potential occurrence of ominous events. A critical difference is in the role that rituals play in these two disorders; BDD rituals are more likely to increase anxiety. Lastly, with BDD, preoccupying thoughts appear to be less intrusive than in OCD.

The Major Issues of Loss Experienced by People with BDD

Two of the major behavioral characteristics of BDD are social avoidance and occupational dysfunction. Social avoidance can become so extreme that people with BDD will isolate themselves from loved ones. In many cases people prefer to stay unmarried, and the loss in such a situation can only be described as severe or major. Harvey and Weber (1998) refer to major loss as, "involving a reduction in a person's resources to which the person is emotionally attached." The act of coping with the actual or potential loss confirms it as real loss. One should not find it difficult to understand the relationship that this statement has with someone with BDD. "Perhaps one of the most daunting aspects of reverberating losses through a lifespan is the recurrent memories associated with the losses." It is in the mental and behavioral revisions (day to day) that the BDD person may wonder, "Who am I anyway?" and this can occupy the person for years, if not a lifetime.

An important aspect of anyone's life in the modern economic world is the necessity to work. It is therefore important that people are physically and mentally able to function in such a way that they can earn a living. Without this ability, life can only be of a degrading nature. Research has found that people with BDD become occupationally dysfunctional and this has a ripple effect to secondary losses. The BDD person may lose self-esteem, self-confidence, and could mentally get into intrapersonal conflict of self-worth.

Options and Procedures for Caring for People with BDD

Diagnostic Criteria for BDD. There are two primary methods available. The first is in terms of the American Psychiatric Association's Diagnostic and Statistical Manual for Mental Disorders (APA, 1994, 445). Therapists should consult the APA for accurate qualifying criteria (APA, 1994):

- Preoccupation with some imagined defect in appearance in a normal-appearing person. (If a slight physical anomaly is present, the person's concern is grossly excessive.)
- The belief in the defect is not of delusional intensity, as in Delusional Disorder, Somatic Type.
- Occurrence is not exclusively during the course of anorexia nervosa or even transsexualism.

The second method is in terms of an interview scale, specific to BDD developed by James Rosen of the University of Vermont. This is an excellent tool for identifying symptoms. It includes questions such as how often the person experiences upsetting preoccupation with appearance, how often the person thought other people were scrutinizing his or her defect, and how often the person camouflages or hides his or her appearance.

Treatment. A combination of pharmacological and psycho-therapeutic treatment is often recommended for people with BDD as there are no controlled outcome studies pertaining to this disorder. Although there are several types of antidepressants available, encouraging results have been recorded with serotonin reuptake inhibitors (SRIs) and cognitive-behavioral treatment (CBT), which may reduce or alleviate signs and symptoms of BDD. These techniques focus on breaking compulsive patterns, such as gazing in the mirror and asking others for reassurance. Social avoidance, on the other hand, is countered by helping people learn to deal with social situations that provoke appearance anxiety. CBT can be successful when used alone while at the same time it is recommended that clients involve their families for social support and understanding.

For optimal treatment of people with BDD, further research and studies are required. Like many other conditions, different treatments are successful for different people. As there is only little empirical information available, therapists must make use of every opportunity to gather data relating to case studies of BDD.

References

American Psychiatric Association. 1994. *Diagnostic and statistical manual of mental disorders*, 4th ed. Washington, DC.

Andreasen, N. C. and J. Bardach. 1977. American Psychiatric Association. *Am J Psychiatry* 134: 673–676.

Barbato, A. and H. J. Irwin. 1992. Major therapeutic systems and the bereavement client. *Australian Psychologist* 27(1): 22–27.

Bonanno, G. A., C. B. Wortman, D. R. Lehman, R. G. Tweed, M. Haring, J. Sonnega, Carr, and R. M. Nesse. 2002. Resilience to loss and chronic grief: A prospective study from preloss to 18-month postloss. *Journal of Personality and Social Psychology* 83(5): 1150–1164.

Bowers, W. A. 2001. Cognitive model of eating disorders. *Journal of Cognitive Psychology: An International Quarterly* 15(4): 331–333.

Clausen, S. 2005. Body dysmorphic disorder: Through a glass darkly. SHO Psychiatry retrieved May 11, 2005 from http://www.studentbmj.com/issues/05/04/education/144.php.

Etcoff, N. 1999. Is beauty an honest signal or a false symbol? *Survival of the prettiest.* New York: Anchor Book.

Harvey, J. H. and A. L. Weber. 1998. Why there must be a psychology of loss: *Perspectives of loss: A sourcebook.* Philadelphia: Brunner-Mazel.

Ladee, G. A. 1966. *Hypochondriacal syndromes.* Amsterdam: Elsevier Publishing Company.

Marks, I. and J. Mishan. 1988. The Royal College of Psychiatrists. *The British Journal of Psychiatry* 152: 674–678.

McLeod, J. 2003. *An introduction to counseling*. Maidenhead: Open University Press.

Murray, J. 2002. Communicating with the community about grieving: A description and a review of the foundations of the broken leg analogy of grieving. *Journal of Loss and Trauma* 7:47–69.

Neimeyer, R. A. 2002. Searching for meaning of meaning: Grief therapy and the process of reconstruction. *Death Studies* 24(6): 541–558.

Neimeyer, R. A. 1999. Narrative strategies in grief therapy. *Journal of Constructivist Psychology* 121: 65–85.

Neimeyer, R. A., and L. A. Gamino. 2003. The experience of grief and bereavement. In *Handbook of death and dying, vol. 2: The response to death*. Thousand Oaks: Sage Publications, Inc.

Rando, T. A. 1993. Clinical assessment of grief and mourning. In *Treatment of complicated mourning*. Champaign: Research Press.

Raphael, B., C. Minkov, and M. Dobson. 2001. Psychotherapeutic and pharmacological intervention for bereaved persons. In *Handbook of bereavement research: Consequences, coping and care*. Washington, DC: American Psychological Association.

Servaty-Seib, H. L. 2004. Connections between counseling theories and current theories of grief and mourning. *Journal of Mental Health Counseling* 26(2): 125–145.

Stroebe, M. 2002. Paving the way: From early attachment theory to contemporary bereavement research. *Mortality*, 7(2): 127–138.

Stroebe, M., M. van Son, W. Stroebe, R. Kleber, H. Schut, and J. van den Bout. 2002. On the classification and diagnosis of pathological grief. *Clinical Psychological Review* 20(1): 57–75.

Thompson, J. K. 2002. Body image and body dysmorphic disorder 1996–2005. Retrieved May 18, 2005 from <u>http://</u> www.athealth.com/Consumer/disorders/BDDInterview. html.

———. (1992) Body dysmorphic disorder: A special case. *Journal of Cognitive Psychology: An International Quarterly* 115(4): 34–44.

Tomita, T., and T. Kitamura. 2002. Clinical and research measures of grief: A reconsideration. *Comprehensive Psychiatry* 43(2): 95–102.

Worden, J. W. 2002. Attachment, loss, and the tasks of mourning. In *Grief counseling and grief therapy: A handbook for the mental health practitioner.* New York: Springer Publishing.

Chapter Seven

Relationship Counseling

SECTION ONE:
Reflecting on Counseling Sessions

Going through notes and reflecting on previous couple's counseling sessions in regard to relationship issues helps me to keep abreast with my own personal development and learning. Each couple brings with them past and present issues pertaining to their situation. In many cases, some have worked through their respective experiences and have lists of things they want to talk about and work through. Many attend sessions with preconceived ideas that they want to negotiate. In many instances, these ideas are totally different from those they negotiated with one another when their relationships first started. What is of utmost importance for counselors is to get their stories before attempting to solve the problem. The *listening* factor appears again.

Example Notes: Relationship Counseling Couples

Conducting the first part of the joint interview with a couple is to find out about their relationship problems and why they sought counseling. It is important to make both persons feel at ease while each counseling session creates a secure and safe environment. Summarizing and reframing their shared stories requires focusing on relationship strengths. This is also the case in determining what previous attempts were made in solving any conflict. Determining whether any commitments were made towards making the relationship work is part of the initial process. Using open questions allows for more constructive discussions while eye contact retains focus on the issues. Chapter thirteen addresses interpersonal skills in more detail. Enough time must be allowed to conduct the first part of the joint interview. To think that all counseling sessions are without some kind of learning curves would be naive.

The initial joint interview, if conducted within the framework of clarifying shared concerns, relationship strengths, commitment to resolve conflict, and identifying previous attempts, should create a sound base to continue the therapeutic process. Establishing rapport with a couple is crucial and will allow for further open discussions necessary to search for causes of distress. Formal assessment questionnaires, such as when communication from one or both parties seems to lack, can serve as valuable tools. It helps to stop one person from blaming the other as well as defusing couple quarrels.

Be alert not to be biased towards one person. Personal values could draw the counselor towards one person's perspective. As counselor, one must feel comfortable about a couple's individual perceptions. Both have their respective views, sometimes in contrast to one another. Evaluate the different meanings that each partner brings to the session. In turn, this can allow one to be objective and to acknowledge that both are part of the therapeutic process. In many cases both persons have psychological hurt. It is in close relationships that we are most at risk of getting hurt. The benefit in the joint counseling approach is that it helps a person that feels hurt to calm down before expressing feelings, express feelings clearly, and keep the size of the event in perspective.

Emotions can allow couples to end up in a negative spiral. Our respective expectations make us see what we want to see as we tend to interpret negatively. In turn, it allows for the conflict to escalate. Understanding the development phases of the person as well as the attachment to a safe and secure environment can help in couple counseling. It is by setting good ground rules that we allow for control and further respectful discussions about our feelings.

The listener-speaker technique is a very useful tool. To listen to a partner speaking is one thing but to hear exactly what they say and what they mean is quite another. Poor listening skills can go nowhere while good listening skills bring better understanding. This also goes for speaking skills. There is huge value in a simple and clear message while a positive tone can only enhance the meaning of what is being communicated. The speaker-listener technique is surely beneficial to both partners when used correctly, especially when it is combined with positive and polite conversation. Positive and polite communication has its benefit but it is necessary to put such talk into action. It brings about new behaviors that will reconcile with the positive language between partners. (For more information see the part of managing conflict between couples under the chapter on treating couples involved in alcohol abuse.)

Problem solving skills training methods have value in couples counseling. However, it will not necessarily be beneficial for all. All emotional conflict should be absent before proceeding with this cognitive approach. Both partners in couple counseling should fully understand the listener-speaker technique before they can partake in any problem solving. As counselor, one must make sure that the timing to engage into problem solving is correct. Therefore, five different stages are crucial to be part of rational and cognitive thinking:

1. Identifying the problem by both
2. Brainstorming between both people
3. Prediction of like consequences
4. Evaluation of solutions
5. Selecting a solution

Cognitive Behavioral Therapy (CBT) has been quite successful in couples therapy. Brief therapy (solution-focused) within the framework of the treatment plan, seems very effective. The difference between an event (a single happening) and issues (underlying, unresolved, conflicting things), which is critical in successful counseling, becomes clearer as one works through the sessions, listening to their stories. The six primary underlying (hidden) issues in couple therapy are power, caring, recognition, commitment, integrity, and acceptance. These hidden issues can control couples and lead conflict to a point of explosion. Equally important matters that sometimes surface are the signs of less obvious behaviors such as wheel spinning, continuous triggers, and avoidance.

Brief self-regulatory couple therapy (things that couples can do without direct help) is a valuable option. Self-regulating therapy it is about setting themselves up to regulate own problems. The counselor prepares the couple to help them progress to the point of self-start. Gains that have been made by the couple can be identified and maintained by themselves.

Parenting and Couple Counseling

With parenting as the primary focus, the counseling session starts with the same approach as with couples. In identifying couple conflict over parenting and low marital satisfaction it is clear that child behavior (differences between couples as how to manage discipline) could sit at the core of the conflict. Although problems can be identified through normal verbal communication, assessment questionnaires are available for identifying specific problems. Should it be necessary to use them, this is often a good option.

While a child's behavior can have a negative impact on parents, couple conflict also has negative impact on children. In this scenario, communication may be an issue. Central to conflict management, the behaviour of both parents and children have negative influences on a relationship. Another factor central to conflict is that of emotions such as anger, sadness, anxiety, and depression. Although there are many more emotional experiences, it is important to clearly identify those behaviors that go along with specific emotions.

Sexual and Marital Issues in Couple Counseling

In regard to the issue of intimacy and sexual behavior in a couple's relationship, counselors must create a climate where everyone feels comfortable discussing it. It is part of the professional process of therapy. Counseling regarding sexual or marital problems focuses on the events and the underlying issues that bring couples for counseling. All relationships go through joyful times, and couples can be guided towards activities they share when relationships go well. By doing this they can re-engage in these shared happy things to bring them closer to one another again. Matters that were not important during their *honeymoon* period may now be viewed differently.

Psycho-education on matters of sexual dysfunction could be relevant. It could be addressed in terms of certain techniques, but only once such issues have been identified as causes, or potential causes, of conflict in the relationship. Such issues may only arise during individual sessions depending on the situation.

SECTION TWO:
Treatment Manual: Counseling Couples Involved in Substance Abuse

Of all drug abuse in Australia, alcohol abuse had been identified as the number one problem. Although this treatment model is based on alcohol abuse, it is equally useful as a treatment manual for any substance abuse in general.

There has been little research into the impact of alcohol on the marital unit. It has become evident that problems within it become intertwined with virtually every other aspect of a couple's life. It is also known that there is a reciprocal relationship between alcohol abuse and marital problems. While clinicians are often confronted by a non-user spouse who wonders why the partner has an alcohol use problem when he or she seemed so normal during the courtship period, researchers have found that users commonly reduce their intake during the first year of marriage. There is no evidence that the *act of marriage* itself institutes a reduced usage or whether a combination of different life events creates changing behavior. Marriage may provide the individual with a drinking partner. Both will adjust their respective behaviors until they match. Should there not be a match, alcohol abuse will have a negative impact on the couple. Furthermore, there is a shift in relationship patterns following marriage; husbands tend to drop friends whose alcohol use does not correspond with their own while they spend less time in social activities.

Developmental Issues

The role played by marital factors in the development and maintenance of problems of alcohol use is considerable. Individuals reared with an alcoholic parent are at risk of developing alcohol problems, both due to genetic factors and faulty role-modeling. This school of thought is supported by Wallen (1993) who writes that an individual's current developmental stage affects how he or she experiences interventions for alcohol abuse. As individuals, couples also undergo developmental stages and developmental tasks. When joining each other in a relationship, both enter into commitment to a new system. Moving through the new system, the couple must complete each developmental task as a unit while simultaneously supporting one another. They adapt moving from one stage to the next as appropriate in establishing the new unit. While marital problems may stimulate excessive alcohol use, couple interactions often help to maintain alcohol-use problems once they have developed. Excessive drinking may provide more subtle adaptive consequences for the couple, such as facilitating the expression of emotion and affection. Thus, the amount of distance and closeness between individuals becomes a ritual. In many instances during recovery, marital conflict may precipitate renewed alcohol abuse by abstinent individuals.

The Marital Dyad, or Twosome, and Substance Abuse

Research found that issues of control are central to the substance-abusing marriage. Both partners try to maintain control and decrease chaos for their own purposes. While the substance-abusing partner may not want the non-user to leave, the latter is also often afraid of abandonment. Conditional love thus becomes a daily part of life. They often communicate through anger and hostility. Couples extensively use projection, forecasting what they believe will happen in the future. They display poor psychological boundaries and blame one another frequently. There is the tendency for these relationships to have a *borderline personality* involving either intense hate or love, being totally in control or totally out of control. These partners are so interrelated that they are inseparable emotionally, psychologically, and sometimes physically from one another and from their drugs of choice.

Co-dependency

Enmeshed or disengaged relationships tend to be highly symbiotic or otherwise known as codependent. The codependent is usually the person closest to the abuser and the first person to react dysfunctionally. As the non-abuser becomes more vulnerable and reactive to the abuser, the abuser increases his or her alcohol consumption. Therefore, the codependent must become more reactive and protective. Being protective does not allow the user to experience the consequences of the behavior. This cycle engages both partners in self-deception and allows the problem to remain hidden. The codependent person is over involved, obsessed over attempting to control the user's behavior, gains self-worth from the approval of others, and makes great sacrifices for others. The non-abusing partner will protect the user partner as much as possible in an effort to maintain the couple homeostasis. This pattern soon becomes a common coping mechanism and is often referred to as *enabling*.

Common Themes in Distressed Relationships

A common element across evidence-based counseling approaches to couple therapy is that they focus on *themes* of couple interaction. Therapists try to identify underlying issues that are common in repeated distressed relationships. There are three dominant areas in couple's interaction themes.

Boundaries. These are the desired levels of closeness versus autonomy within a relationship. *Low* boundaries indicate a high level of desired intimacy. *High* boundaries indicate high levels of autonomy and independence. The relationship between the alcohol abusing client and his or her spouse can be perceived as analogous to the client's relationship with his or her family of origin. Unresolved conflicts are displaced and acted within the marital relationship in an attempt to assert autonomy and submitting, often resentfully, to what are perceived as the demands or needs of the spouse.

Power and control. The decisions that partners make will have a substantial impact on both. They need to find a way in which to distribute power and control in the relationship. Often it is only when the symptomatic behavior of the alcohol abuser becomes severe, that the spouse expresses concern about the person's well-being.

Investment. The degree of commitment and effort each partner makes falls into two domains. Firstly, those who are emotionally (intimacy between partners) connected and secondly, those who are instrumental (investment in the daily household chores).

Goals for Couples Therapy with Alcohol Abusers

At the time when the alcohol abuser has decided to change his or her drinking habit, couples therapy has two basic areas to be tackled in order to stabilize short-term change: the drinking problem and the marriage relationship.

First Goal. The first goal is to reduce or eliminate abusive drinking and to help the drinker's efforts to change. The focus is on changing *alcohol-related interactional patterns* such as nagging about past drinking but ignoring current sober behavior. Couples are encouraged to engage in behaviors more pleasing to each other. Continual reference to past and future drinking problems may lead to renewed drinking. It can also lead to the alcohol abuser feeling more discouraged about the relationship, which in turn could result in less pleasing behavior.

Second Goal. The second goal involves altering general relationship patterns to make provision for an atmosphere that is more conducive to sobriety. In this phase the couple is supported to repair the often extensive damage incurred during past conflict about alcohol. It further involves helping them find solutions to difficulties that may not be directly related to the alcohol problem. The couple must learn about, confront, and resolve relationship conflicts without the alcohol abuser resorting to drinking.

Clients Most Likely to Benefit

O'Farrell (1993) points out those studies examining predictors of response to behavioral marital treatment and other couples therapy with alcoholics. Factors that predict the alcoholic's acceptance and completion of therapy provide some information on clients most likely to benefit from treatment. These clients must stay in therapy to benefit. Those clients most likely to benefit from therapy often have the following characteristics:

- A high school or better qualification
- Employed full-time if able and desirous to work
- Older
- Are willing to stay together for the duration of the therapeutic course
- Engage in therapy directly after a crisis, especially one that threatens the stability of the relationship
- The spouse and other family members are not alcoholic
- The alcoholic, spouse, and other family members are without serious psychopathology or drug abuse
- Absence of family violence that has caused serious injury or is potentially life-threatening

Willingness to actively partake in therapeutic treatment and a desire to change behavior are also contributing factors towards a successful outcome. Clients who reflect these characteristics are more likely to benefit.

Necessary Counselor Attributes

Certain counselor attributes and behaviors are critical for successful couples counseling:

- All treatment must be structured so that control of the alcohol abuse is the first priority, before attempting to support the couple with any other problems. The hope that reduction in relationship distress will lead to improvement in the drinking problem is rarely fulfilled.

- Helping the couple defuse their intense anger and their blaming of one another is very important.

- Taking control of treatment sessions, especially during early assessment and therapy requires structure and control by the therapist. The rules of the treatment must be clearly established and enforced from the outset of the treatment. The therapist can use empathic listening to help each member to feel they have been heard. The therapist should insist that only one person speak at a time.

- The therapist needs to take a long-term view of the course of change. Both alcohol abuse and relationship distress may reduce only by repeated efforts. A long-term view may help the counselor encounter relapse without becoming overly discouraged. The counselor should keep in contact with the couple long after the problems have been stabilized.

Initiating Change and Helping the Spouse

Therapists often have initial *gut* reactions that include feelings of vicarious helplessness and desire to tell people to get out of the relationship. Such inclinations are usually not helpful, especially when they are hopeful that the alcohol-abuser could change his or her drinking habits. Besides the importance of an empathic response, the therapist has two general guidelines to follow. First, the non-drinker is told that they are not responsible for the drinking problem. Secondly, that they cannot make the drinker change as they are not in control of the problem. Following on from this the therapist helps the spouse to identify those elements that he or she is in control of. The following are important elements of encouragement:

- Take care of them first
- Decide how much negativity they are willing to live with
- Decide what they are not willing to live with
- Consider individual therapy or engage in self-help groups
- Don't argue with the person who has been drinking in order to lessen potential violence
- Take advantage of windows of motivation such as willingness to enter treatment

It is important to assist the non-user to strengthen his or her coping capabilities, to enhance couple and family functioning, and to facilitate greater sobriety on the part of the alcohol abuser. Unilateral Family Therapy provides a series of graded steps the spouse can use prior to confrontation. Although these steps can be useful in their own rights, they can also pave the way for positive outcome. The therapist emphasizes the following:

- The non-user is not to blame
- Potential of the spouse to become a rehabilitative influence
- Importance to enhance the relationship by engaging in behaviors pleasing to the drinker when he or she is sober
- Importance to refrain from enabling or trying to control the drinking

Motivating an Initial Commitment to Change in the Alcohol Abuser

For the individual who is not yet willing to stop drinking, a marital therapy approach will try to help the spouse to motivate the uncooperative, denying alcoholic to change behavior. Vernon Johnson (Hester and Miller 1989) of the Johnson Institute of Minneapolis developed a widely-known and used intervention procedure that involves three or four educational and rehearsal sessions with the non-user prior to the intervention itself. The alcohol-abuser is confronted and strongly encouraged to engage in treatment. The goal of interviewing the non-user is to do the following:

- Establish an alliance
- Enhance motivation
- Determine the areas of difficulties the partner's drinking has caused
- Determine what attempts have in the past been made to help stop the drinking
- Determine what attempts have in the past been successful (Hester and Miller 1989)

Assessment of Alcohol-Use Problems

Overview of Assessment. The two most common errors in the assessment of couples are doing too little or too much. On the one hand, too little assessment leads to commencing treatment with an inadequate understanding of the couple, often without the couple feeling understood. In turn this often leads to inappropriate intervention and poor couple engagement in the therapeutic process. On the other hand, too much assessment wastes everybody's time and often makes couples feel that irrelevancies are being dragged into the process. Core assessment tasks include joint interviews, individual interviews, self-report inventories, self-monitoring tasks, and behavioral tasks.

The goal of the assessment process is to develop a shared understanding between the couple and the therapist. Working towards understanding is to promote positive change and at the same time the therapist reflects the information back to the couple. Sharing the information in this way helps in building empathy. The accuracy of the information is continuously checked during counseling. This is done through reframing and summarizing.

Assessing the couple. Reciprocity marriage counseling is a set of procedures designed to teach couples how to communicate better. Assessments can be used with couples, roommates, people who are dating, and with gay or lesbian couples. At the start of all sessions have both clients complete a questionnaire aimed at producing a marriage happiness rating. Their respective happiness with various categories of their life in the relationship will show on a ten-point scale. This assessment will guide the therapist and both partners to the situation at the time of the evaluation.

In the first few sessions, the counselor will mainly be concentrating on putting clients at ease, allowing them to feel that they are being given time to express their respective stories. This is when the counselor has the opportunity to form a relationship and to create trust between the counselor and the clients. When the clients feel that their way of seeing the world is understood and remembered in the counseling process, that their hopes and fears are being listened to, the chance of helping them has increased. This happens for several reasons. First, knowledge of the client's situation can only emerge when he or she feels safe enough to explore it. Second, only when this relatively relaxed explanation has taken place will the counselor be able to form a hypothesis of what the problem may be. Third, when people are at ease, their own problem-solving ability is greatly heightened. The result is that the counselor and the couple are working together rather than against one another towards a positive outcome.

While the counselor builds on the trusting alliance with the couple, the initial inquiries usually tend to be around the specific problem. Matters of specific focus include the following:

- The help the couple has had with their problem
- How long the problem has persisted
- Factors perpetuating the problem
- Current major life issues
- How the couple interacts together
- The couple's social and cultural context
- Each partner's physical and mental health, both currently and in the past
- Each partner's family experience
- Legal proceedings in hand
- Other helpers or agencies involved
- Significant interactions concerning the couple that is not apparent
- Significant third parties involved in the relationship
- Case notes; the amount of available other related information

Assessing the Alcohol Abuser. The most important and critical session is the first. It is during this session that the groundwork is laid to motivate the client by providing him or her with the potential of a successful outcome. The client tends to bring in someone they feel cares about them and will support them in the counseling process. They may be motivated to stop drinking because they have just done something that they dislike while intoxicated. Whatever the motivation, it is important for the therapist to understand the reasons. These reasons can be used as counter mechanisms to keep the client sober. The importance of the first session is reflected in the prime question. *Why did you decide to do something about your drinking problem now?* The therapist must also ensure that the client is informed that the therapist will interview the significant other alone during the course of the counseling process.

Assessment is more than a one-time paperwork task for the therapist. It is in fact the first step in the rehabilitation process. The most researched diagnostic instrument for assessing alcohol abuse is the self-administered Michigan Alcoholism Screening Test (MAST). (Consult a counselor on the availability of this assessment.) The twenty-five item questionnaire identifies up to 95 percent of alcoholics. MAST may realistically and effectively be used with virtually any population group. Clients are instructed to answer all questions either *yes* or *no*. After completion of the test, the points assigned to each question are totaled. A total of four points is presumptive evidence of alcoholism whereas a total of five points or more makes it extremely unlikely that the individual is not an alcoholic. A further three questions from the MAST can be used to quickly assess potential alcoholic problems: Has your spouse ever objected to your drinking? Do you ever think you drink too much in general? Have others ever said you drink too much for your own good?

These three questions can easily be incorporated into the interview process to serve as indicators for a follow-up detailed assessment. Additional to the MAST, there is also a shortened version namely the Short Michigan Alcoholism Screening Test (SMAST), which consists of only thirteen of twenty-five questions taken from MAST.

The CAGE assessment is another form of evaluation for adults and is a four-item questionnaire. It includes questions related to a history of attempting to *cut* down on alcoholic intake (C), *annoyance* over criticism about alcohol (A), *guilt* about drinking behavior (G), and drinking first thing in the morning to relieve withdrawal anxiety, sometimes referred to as an *eye-opener* (E). Use of the CAGE questions effectively distinguishes alcoholics from non-alcoholics at or above 90 percent. The client is asked to answer *yes* or *no* to the following four questions: Have you ever tried to cut down on your drinking? Are you annoyed when people ask you about your drinking? Do you ever feel guilty about your drinking? Do you ever take a morning eye-opener?

Only *yes* answers are scored on the CAGE. One yes indicates a possibility of alcoholism; two or three indicate a high alcohol suspicion index and four answers of yes indicate that alcoholism is highly likely.

Physical and Psychological Complications of Alcohol Abuse

Not only does the abuse of alcohol affect a couple's relationship, but excessive alcohol abuse affects particularly all organ systems in the body at different stages. One method for categorizing the medical complications of alcohol abuse is to describe its chronic, acute and withdrawal effects. For further medical information, please see Lowinson et al. (2004) *Substance Abuse* and for information pertaining to Jellinek's *Three Phases of Alcoholism* see Maxman and Ward (1995).

Chronic effects. Perhaps the best-known chronic effect of heavy drinking is liver disease. This disease can manifest in three forms: fatty liver, liver cirrhosis and Korsakoff's syndrome. The main impairment associated with chronic effects is related to memory disturbance. It is the inability to learn new information or to recall previously learned information.

Acute effects. Acute effects of alcohol abuse depend on the time course of drinking. During the initial period, of up to thirty minutes after drinking even a small amount, there is typically mood elevation, followed by sedative and anxiolytic effects. Maladaptive behavior or psychological behavior changes present through inappropriate sexual or aggressive behavior, mood liability, impaired judgement, impaired social, or occupational functioning develop shortly after alcohol ingestion.

Alcohol withdrawal. Chronic heavy alcohol abusers who abstain from alcohol for more than a few hours can experience withdrawal symptoms. At its most extreme, withdrawal can produce the syndrome of delirium tremens, which occurs between twenty-four and forty-eight hours after alcohol cessation. They are a form of clouding of consciousness and vivid visual hallucinations.

Co-morbidity. Alcohol abuse often occurs with other addictive and psychiatric disorders. Nicotine dependence is the highest. It also occurs commonly with addiction to narcotics. Up to 89 percent of cocaine-dependent people are also dependent on alcohol. An interesting feature of co-morbidity of alcohol with other addictive substances is that the association is greatest for those with the youngest age of onset of problem drinking. Individuals with alcohol dependence also tend to have high rates of co-morbidity with other disorders. The more notable association appears to be with a variety of affective and anxiety-related behaviors:

- Up to 67 percent of alcohol abusers have major depression
- As many as 60 percent of individuals with bipolar disorder either abuse or are addictive to alcohol
- Rates of alcohol abuse are as high as 63 percent among those with anxiety disorder
- As many as 64 percent have post-traumatic stress disorder
- Antisocial personality disorder is common among those who develop problem drinking habits early in life, up to 8 percent
- Rates are also elevated among people who suffer from schizophrenia

The Treatment Process

Therapy for couples invoved in alcoholism is always a transition, always moving from one stage to another. Every part or event is influenced by many factors such as hidden issues that only surface from time to time during the process. The couple therapy process according to Barker (1984) consists of at least seven overlapping developmental phases which people go through to achieve their goals.

Preliminary facilitation. This first phase of couple therapy consists of an exchange of as much relevant information between counselor and couple as possible before their first one-on-one contact.

Initial Encounter. During this phase the counselor's primary objective is to help the couple become engaged in treatment.

Goal setting. Goal setting is listing outcome goals, process goals or methods of achieving them, and defining the treatment plan.

Overcoming resistance. People are generally uncomfortable about changes even when their current circumstances cause them discomfort.

Implementing functional change. This phase might appear to be the heart of intervention as it has the longest lasting of all phases. It consists of four therapy activities, namely:

- Interview strategies that help couples understand themselves and their relationship
- A working relationship, which helps them experience, understand and explore their feelings
- Tasks that are assigned to the couple by the counselor
- The counselor assumes different roles to achieve relevant understanding and behavioral changes

Termination. The way termination occurs can negate or solidify any gains made in counseling.

Follow-up. It is necessary to follow-up on homework assigned to the couple. As there is no single best or worst way, the better solution is to suit the unique needs and circumstances of each couple.

The Community Reinforced Approach

The Community Reinforced Approach (CRA) to the treatment of alcohol abuse is a set of behavioral-based treatment procedures developed by George Hunt and Nathan Azrin in 1973. It enables the client to have a more meaningful life without alcohol. Originally, it was designed for inpatients only. However, with ongoing improvements, it became possible to treat people on an outpatient basis. The treatment procedures included spouses encouraging

J AMES DE BEER

their partners to seek treatment as early as possible. The CRA program includes the following components:

- A prescription for disulfiram (Antabuse)
- A motivational program to encourage the client to continue to take disulfiram
- Reciprocity couple counseling
- A job club for unemployed clients
- Social skills training programs
- Advocacy on social and recreational activities
- Help with cravings and urges

Although the alcohol-Antabuse reaction can make people extremely ill, it is a safe medication when the person is well informed. Prior arrangements with a local doctor who understands alcohol abuse will be very helpful. In this way the client can almost immediately start using Antabuse without any further delay. For people without any social support, it is important to have developed such an environment from the start of the treatment.

To effectively implement the CRA program, a number of systems should be established before the counselor starts to see clients using this approach:

- Try to see the client on the same day that he or she makes the decision to engage in the treatment
- Inpatients are to be seen as early as possible during the start of the treatment
- Clients must be encouraged to bring someone of significance with them
- Once the client has made the decision to take Antabuse, he or she must see a physician

- The client must take the Antabuse under optimal conditions

Furthermore, the necessity of interviewing the partner of the alcohol abuser is critically important. Reciprocity couple counseling helps the couple to communicate better because often couples stop communicating positively and keep things inside when they drink heavily. The issue of communication will be discussed in more detail under the heading *Resolving Conflicts and Problems*.

Drink-refusal training, social and recreational counseling, and controlling cravings and urges are also part of the CRA program and is being discussed under the heading *Cravings and Urges*.

Alcoholics Anonymous (AA)

Since its founding by Dr. Bob Smith and Bill Wilson on June 10, 1935, Alcoholics Anonymous (AA) has grown into a worldwide organization with an estimated two million active members in almost ninety-seven thousand groups in more than one hundred countries. AA has influenced, guided, and shaped the treatment of alcohol abuse. It would be difficult to find an alcohol abuse program that does not include the principles of AA. The program consists of studying and following their *Twelve Steps*. It also includes the *Twelve Traditions* which groups are careful to adhere to. The Twelve Steps listed below offer the alcohol abuser a sober way of life.

The Twelve Steps of AA

1. We admitted we were powerless over alcohol—that our lives had become unmanageable.

2. Came to believe that a Power greater than ourselves could restore us to sanity.
3. Made a decision to turn our will and our lives over to the care of God *as we understood Him.*
4. Made a searching and fearless moral inventory of ourselves.
5. Admitted to God, to ourselves and to another human being the exact nature of our wrongs.
6. Were entirely ready to have God remove all these defects of character.
7. Humbly ask Him to remove our shortcomings.
8. Made a list of all persons we had harmed, and became willing to make amends to them all.
9. Made direct amends to such people wherever possible, except when to do so would injure them or others.
10. Continued to take personal inventory and when we were wrong promptly admitted it.
11. Sought through prayer and meditation to improve our conscious contact with God, *as we understood Him,* praying only for knowledge of His will for us and the power to carry that out.
12. Having had a spiritual awakening as a result of these steps, we tried to carry this message to alcoholics, and to practice these principles in all our affairs.

Narcissistic problems that may be observed in alcohol abusers include the belief that they can take care of problems themselves. Also that they are self-sufficient and that they are able to retain the necessary control over alcohol and other areas of their lives. Therefore, defiance and grandiosity stand in the way of the alcohol abuser's surrender, and result in fleeting states of compliance but not a real acceptance of defeat at the hands of alcohol. Lowinson et al. (2004) state that how AA works, how well, and for whom, remain unsatisfactorily researched.

Further studies of the AA program are available in Galanter and Kleber (2001). Here are some recommended areas:

- The Twelve Traditions
- What AA promises
- What AA does not do
- Group process
- Ego functions
- Pathologic narcissism
- Empathic understanding
- Spiritual dimension
- Accepting limitations
- Mental health professions and AA
- The differences between AA and psychiatry

Cravings and Urges

Important concepts. Researchers agree that cravings and urges are important concepts in treatment. However, there is no accepted universal definition, nor is there a way to measure them. Craving is an intense subjective emotional and physical experience that varies from person to person. Urges are of less intensity and are viewed as a cognitive experience.

Coping with cravings and urges. Cravings and urges go hand in hand with habits. The initial days of a habit-kicking plan can be exhausting as urges and cravings dominate thinking and interfere with daily routine.

When will the cravings go? Each recovering person is different. For some, cravings cease when they quit. For the majority, the urge loses its bulldog grip gradually day by day during the first year. Realization of disappearing cravings and urges can come suddenly, whereafter they can stay away forever.

What if they don't go away after one year? If cravings and urges do not go away after one year, it's time to get extra help. Consider seeing a counselor who specializes in addictions or a doctor specializing in alcohol and drug abuse. Consider in- or out-patient treatment. Living with cravings for a long period of time can be pretty miserable; it could cause relapse.

Controlling cravings and urges. To resist cravings, it helps to consider why you feel them. They come on for various reasons: e.g., fear for the withdrawal symptoms or the longing for the rush of a high. Cravings are irrational but powerful enough to overcome rational thoughts. You can reduce the number of cravings by learning to thwart temptations by keeping your lifestyle in balance.

Communication and Conflict Management

Listener speaker skills. Inadequate communication is a major problem for couples involved in alcohol abuse. The inability to resolve conflicts can cause abusive drinking and severe couple tension to recur. The training of communication skills starts by defining effective communication as message intended (by speaker) equals message received (by listener). Each individual needs to learn both listening and speaking skills while the therapist can use instructions, modeling, prompting, behavioral rehearsal, and feedback to teach couples how to communicate more effectively.

Learning these skills is an essential prerequisite for problem solving and negotiating desired behavior changes. Sessions are planned and structured so spouses can talk privately, face to face and without any distractions. Each person takes a turn to be the speaker expressing his or her point of view without interruptions, then to be the listener of the other party's view. *Listening skills* help each spouse to feel understood and supported. It slows down couple interactions to prevent quick escalation of aversive exchange. *Speaker skills* help to express both positive and negative feelings directly. The speaker is taught to communicate clearly as an alternative to blaming, hostile, and indirect communication; these are behaviors that characterize many alcohol abuse couples.

Problem solving skills. Problem solving has been a cornerstone for management of conflict in couples. It involves teaching couples a set of rational decision-making steps, which are intended to help the couple negotiate decisions. Problem solving is useful when two preconditions are met: Firstly, the couple is emotionally ready to collaborate and secondly, the conflict is about a complex decision that is likely to be resolved by negotiated behavioral change. Furthermore, it helps to define a problem in a mutually acceptable, constructive manner. The therapist promptly helps shape active listening of each partner to the other. Once the partners have developed in their respective communication skills, they are supported to implement self-regulating problem solving management.

SECTION THREE:
Counseling Couples Involved in Obesity Issues

Obesity shares many of the most salient features of addictions. Food is a substance used both repetitively and destructively by either its prolonged restriction or episodic over-consumption. Obesity is in the United States the most chronic disease, affecting more than 25 percent of its population. There is also an increase in obesity in Europe, Australia, New Zealand, the Middle East, and South America. Many suffer from an array of serious weight-related disorders.

Research on relationship interactions in the process of dietary change has found that roles, rules, communication, and flexibility among cohesive, enmeshed, and disengaged couples vary considerably. Conflict between partners becomes evident in their respective behaviors. While communication with enmeshed couples is moderately sustainable, disengaged couples are sustained by poor communication and limited ability to negotiate.

Life course transitions such as marriage or cohabitation are also associated with changes in food choice that may impact on health and body weight. Furthermore, it is the shared lives of couples that are important rather than the existence or absence of a legal relationship.

Developmental Issues Pertaining to People in Relationships

Like individuals, couples also undergo developmental stages as well as developmental tasks. When joining each other in a relationship, both enter into commitment to a new system. Moving through the new system, the couple must complete each developmental task as a unit. Simultaneously, they support one another in adapting and moving from one stage to the next as appropriate in establishing the new unit.

In a survey done with individual members of couples three months prior to cohabitation and again three months after the moving-in date, food-related habits included new approaches to shopping. It also showed new habits on sharing the evening meal together. While compromises were made in order to ensure that both parties ate and enjoyed the same meal, such shared choices may not always have been beneficial. It was also reported that sharing temptation could serve to reduce guilt associated with excess consumption. When it came to food choices, most couples reported that health and weight philosophies influenced patterns and food choice that contributed to food conflicts.

The Attachment Model and its Relevance in Relationships

Lack of energy, the over-weight status of one person, the immobility of one in an intimate relationship, and weight-related habits can lead to differences in the level of intimacy. These differences would feel strange to either partner. It results in a cycle of ongoing struggle around attachment and is exhausting to both. The inherent insecurity makes it difficult for the couple to grow in their relationship. Signs that could help the counselor identify that the attachment model may help include the following:

- Attachment issues as part of the presenting problem such as separations, affairs and desertion
- Recurrent pattern of losses in life such as redundancies, separations and moves
- Involvement in very structured work (e.g., armed forces or nursing) or very lonely work (e.g., long-distance driving)
- Frequent references to concepts such as commitment, rejections, and loss
- Difficulties over partings and meetings
- Anxious attachment shown by notes, phone calls or detachment shown by missed sessions

It may be helpful for the counselor to do one or more of the following:

- Examine the couple's expectations around bonding
- Consciously address the effect of past losses and separation
- Use behavioral tasks to improve partings and meetings
- Create more realistic scenarios around rejection
- Uncover and mourn past unacknowledged losses
- Model safety and security in the arrangement of sessions

Body Image, Self-Esteem, and Weight-Related Criticism from Romantic Partners

Our appearance communicates much more than just physical attributes. Negative perceptions of one's body have been found to be strongly related to low self-esteem. Compared to their less attractive counterparts, people perceived as attractive are viewed as being more socially skilled, popular, happy, confident, intelligent, warm, and well adjusted.

Weight-related teasing from romantic partners potentially compounds the already sensitive body image of women. Feedback from romantic partners may be especially relevant as women in particular strive to match their actual figure to the ideal figure they perceive their partner to hold.

The Association Between Close Relationships and Chronic Illness

According to Halford and Markman (1997) a chronic illness in one spouse affects not only the other spouse, but the relationship in general. There are mainly three areas of importance to researchers in the domain of chronic illness. Kowal and Johnson (2003) describe these areas and their respective relationships with couples as follows:

Relationship status. Married couples tend to show greater compliance to medical regimes, while separated or divorced partners experience lower immune function. They also show lower mortality rates as well as higher survival rates once a chronic illness is diagnosed.

Relationship quality. Marital distress is associated with reduced immune system function, which in turn is associated with physical illness, disease, and compromised health.

Relationship behaviors. Conflict and criticism are among the most important risk factors for unhealthy relationships.

The treatment process. Couple therapy is a process. It is always a transition, always moving from one stage to another and every part or event is influenced by many others such as hidden issues that only surface from time to time during the process. The couple therapy process according to Barker (1984) consists of at least seven overlapping developmental phases.

Aims with Eating-Disorder Couples

Common therapeutic aims with eating-disordered couples are fourfold:

- To disengage the couple from their focus on the symptom
- To provide them with an opportunity for exploring other issues in the marital relationship which have been obscured by their attention to the symptoms of the eating-disorder

- To allow the couple to decide whether they each wish to work on effecting changed behavior on those issues about which they are concerned
- To offer the obese client aid in symptom management. This could range from medical treatment to physical exercise additional to counseling

Treatment Goals

To live with purpose and have goals in general make life meaningful, and although we know human behavior is goal-oriented, many people do not set conscious goals. Treatment goals may vary as a function of the assessment of the couple's strengths and deficits (e.g., interest in cycling or walking as strengths can be used to enhance physical activities). For the majority of couples with relatively midrange dysfunction, a useful goal is to observe integrative capacity in the spouses (e.g., the ability of one spouse to motivate the other; a capacity of motivation).

References

Anderson, A. S., D. W. Marshall, and E. J. Lea. 2003. *Shared lives: An opportunity for obesity prevention?* United Kingdon: University of Dundee Centre for Public Health Nutrition Research.

Azrin, N. H., R. W. Sisson, R. Meyers, and M. Godley. 1982. Alcoholism treatment by disulfiram and community reinforcement therapy. *Journal of Behavior Therapy and Experimental Psychiatry* 13: 105–112.

Barker, R. L. 1984. *Treating couples in crisis: Fundamentals and practice in marital therapy.* New York: The Free Press.

Butler, C., and V. Joyce. 1998. *Counseling couples in relationships: An introduction to the relate approach.* Cornwell: TJ International, Ltd.

Cox, M. 1987. *Treatment and prevention of alcohol problems: A resource manual.* Florida: Academic Press.

Doweiko, H. E. (2006). *Concepts of chemical dependency* (6th ed.). Pacific Grove, CA: Brooks/Cole.

Galanter, M., and H. D. Kleber. 2001. *Textbook of substance abuse treatment, 2nd ed.* New York: The American Psychiatric Press.

Gurman, A. S., D. P. Kniskern. 1978. Deteriation in marital and family therapy: Empirical, Clinical and Conceptional Issues. *Family Process* 17:3–20.

Halford, W. K. 2001. *Brief therapy for couples: Helping partners help themselves.* New York: Guilford Press.

Halford, W. K., and H. J. Markman, eds. 1997. *Clinical handbook of marriage and couples interventions.* Somerset: Bookcraft Ltd.

Hester, R. K., and W. R. Miller, eds. 1989. *Handbook of Alcoholism Treatment: Effective Alternatives.* New York: Pergamon Press.

Jacobson, N. S., and A. S. Gurman. 1986. *Clinical handbook of marital therapy.* New York: The Guilford Press.

Lowinson, J. H., P. Ruiz, R. B. Millman, and J. G.Langrod. 2004. *Substance abuse: A comprehensive textbook,* 4th ed. Versailles: Quebecor World.

Maisto, S. A., T. J. O'Farrell, G. J. Connors, J. McKay, and M. A. Pelcovitz. 1988. Alcoholics' attributions of factors affecting their relapse to drinking and reasons for terminating relapse events. *Addictive Behaviors* 13: 79–82.

Maxmen, J. S., and N. G. Ward. 1995. *Essential psychopathology and its treatment,* 2nd ed. New York: W. W. Norton and Company.

O'Farrell, T. J. 1993. *Treating alcohol problems: Marital and family interventions.* New York: Guilford Press.

Stevens, P., and R. L. Smith. 2005. *Substance abuse counseling: Theory and practice.* Galliard: Phoenix Color Book Group.

Wallen, J. 1993. Addiction in human development: *Developmental perspectives on addiction and recovery.* New York: Haworth Press.

Chapter Eight

Binge Drinking Among Young People

The world we hope to find through binge drinking often comes with huge and costly consequences. The harm caused by alcohol abuse has an impact on every level of society. It stretches from personal misery to social mayhem. A report compiled in 2003 for the Australian Parliament's House of Representatives on substance abuse in Australia states that among 85 percent of Australians, alcohol is the most widely used substance. The World Health Organization (WHO) issued a report in 1996 stating that 11 percent of boys and girls in Australian secondary schools, aged twelve to seventeen years, had engaged in hazardous drinking.

Identifying and reducing the causes of these problems have proven to be somewhat difficult. However, in the school of counseling treatment is available. One such counseling approach is called the *Biopsychosocial Model*. It is a combination of supporting disciplines working with a client at the same time. While the client adheres to medication as described and monitored by the GP, the client engages in counseling and is guided into the social arena.

As in the process of counseling couples involved in alcohol

abuse, in one-on-one counseling the first step is to focus on abstinence. If the client is unable or unwilling to work towards abstinence then the focus is for the client to reduce his or her alcohol use. Should there be any psychiatric symptoms present, the next step is to get the client to engage in psychiatric treatment. This will help to stabilize the condition. The third step is for the client to get involved in social and physical activities while both the counselor and the client work towards positive lifestyle change. Follow-up sessions will focus on progress as well as monitoring relapse. This process was followed with Anna in the first case example.

In case example two, the counseling process with Caron was conducted through CBT, Emotion Focused Therapy, Rational Emotive Therapy (RET), and Gestalt Therapy. During counseling sessions the pendulum swings from working with and through emotions to rational thinking with the purpose to change behavior, thoughts, and feelings, and sometimes talking directly to the absent person in the empty chair.

Case Example One: Anna

Anna, a twenty-year-old single woman requested external counseling while she was undergoing in-house rehabilitation for alcohol dependence. She was at a drug and alcohol rehabilitation centre in Queensland, Australia. She was struggling with giving up alcohol as well as with low self-worth and self-doubts, which was exacerbated by her drinking. Anna said that she did not want to be who she was; she did not want to look at herself in the mirror. She believed that drinking helped her to numb her real world. Her daily routine was staying at home when she was not working. "I had my first drink when I woke up in the morning, be it before four o'clock or earlier." She was drinking about 750ml to 1 liter of vodka mixed with fruit juice per day. Anna suffered from sleeplessness, which often resulted in very early morning drinking sprees. She was paranoid about everyone around her and she often found herself with obsessive thoughts. This, according to her, manifested into panic attacks which she had no control over. Anna acted violently when intoxicated, with frequent suicidal ideation with no specific plans to take her life. Although she got very angry with her supports at times, she had no intent or plan to harm them.

Anna started drinking at the age of sixteen years. She also smoked cannabis but stopped when she became dependent on alcohol. She recalled the time when she started to drink daily. Although Anna believed that she was in control of her drinking she stated that she never liked who she was and that drinking allowed her to be who she could be. Experiencing cravings lead to stealing alcohol, which in turn resulted in her being prosecuted for small crimes.

Anna presented history consistent with a past major depressive episode, experiencing insomnia and panic attacks. Her worst enemy according to her was herself "I do not like who or what I am; I wish I could be someone else." Anna recalled making attempts on her life with acts of self-harm, hitting her head against the floor while kicking objects in and around the house. She often appeared to be aggressive towards close friends and immediate supports such as her housemates. She was not aware of physically hurting them.

Anna had been living with her mother, stepfather, and younger brother in a family house until she moved out into her own rental place. She shared this house with her younger brother and a girl friend. She was in contact with her older married sister who lived outside her local town. Anna had contact with her biological father who lived locally. However, she did not see him or the rest of the family on a regular basis. They did not seem able to help her with her alcohol abuse problem.

Although all Anna's family members, excluding her biological father, engaged in social drinking there did not seem to be any patterns, direct information, or signs of addiction to alcohol use to the same level that she had been experiencing. Anna's behavior of isolation did not seem to have had any connection to the social behavior of her immediate family members. According to her, they interacted in wider circles of friendship and other social activities such as playing sport, cycling, and golf.

Anna's continuous drinking and isolation since the age of about sixteen years had limited her personal development and social development. Her level of reasoning and emotional maturity did not measure to the age of the average twenty-year-old. She left school at fifteen years and had since been doing jobs off and on for the purpose of earning income only. Anna showed no desire for any career development. She was involved in a personal relationship for some six months, which ended in separation. She had subsequently shown no interest in a similar relationship with a male at all.

Two years ago Anna, due to the influence of her biological father, converted to Christianity. Since then she had been active in church attendance and activities and had a good relationship with the pastor and church members. She did not partake or engage in any physical exercise or activities in any way or form. Her life at home had being arranged around her drinking habit, which in turn was engineered to suit her working hours and working conditions. Anna was aware of the impact that her drinking had on her job; however, her working history had shown patterns of high job turnover. She preferred not to socialize during her private time when she occupied herself with her cat. She often obsessively cleaned the house. When drunk, she showed high and low mood levels that manifested in aggression and emotional talk, anxiety, sleeplessness and anger. Although prescription drugs had been suggested by a psychiatrist as well as her family GP she choose not to adhere to the treatment. Anna's violent behavior had escalated since she completed her in-house rehabilitation course; the last act resulted in self-harm by cutting her wrists with a piece of glass from a broken bottle.

Progress of Interviews

Motivational Interviewing: This counseling approach entails four different elements which in short are: the principle of expressing empathy, the principle of rolling with resistance, the principle of searching for "self-change talk," and establishing an alliance with the client.

Motivation to change. Building on self-esteem would help her look for the person she would like to be and strive for fulfillment and integration.

Building rapport and trust. The client is encouraged by reflecting empathy with the following:

- Changing her perception of the personal values (in small steps)
- The probability of achieving successful outcome
- Understanding of environmental barriers and supports that inhibit change (help her to gain confidence)
- Feelings (emotional fitness) helping her to firstly feel safe
- Helping her towards self-efficacy

- Her taking control of her anger
- Cognition behaviors
- Goal setting
- Managing anxiety
- Understanding withdrawal symptoms
- Relapse prevention (Perkinson 2004)
- Motivation for psychiatric assessment (did realize)

The client can also be motivated to engage in biopsychosocial (combined medical, psychological, and social) therapy through the following:

- In-house rehabilitation due to previous success
- Adherence to SSRI and multi-vitamin treatment as pre-scribed by psychiatrist
- Continuous church activities and socialization
- Continuous counseling
- Engaging in physical exercise and outdoor activities

I have subsequently counseled Anna seventeen times. These seventeen sessions included nine counseling sessions during the period that she was undergoing rehabilitation.

One afternoon at work, after not having had any alcohol for ninety-seven days, Anna experienced severe cravings that she found very difficult to control. Although she was aware of the relapse prevention procedures, she could not take control of her urge to drink. She managed to get hold of a bottle of vodka by ordering it from a bottle shop and had it delivered to her work-place. She secretly, she thought, started drinking again. Anna stated that at first it was with an awareness of her situation with the employer and she kept her drinking low key at work. She also stated that she withheld telling me about it for a short while; this was until she noticed that through certain questions I showed suspicion.

I was very disappointed at Anna's relapse after ninety-seven days and nine sessions. It happened at a time when she felt good about her progress. Relapse in alcohol abuse shows that many clients have problems in early sobriety. Their alcohol abuse is likely to increase rather than decrease. The relapse obviously did not meet my expectations.

During her period of sobriety, Anna often showed numerous warning signs that could have lead to potential relapse. Behaviors, such as isolating herself at home when she was not working caused extreme moments of loneliness. During counseling sessions, Anna argued with a sense of tunnel vision. She often showed signs of depression. She had in the past mentioned suicide but without any evidence of a plan or a method. This was dealt with and confirmed through psychiatric assessment and medical treatment.

Being aware of Anna's work schedule and her drinking patterns, a meeting was scheduled with her and her pastor. The meeting was scheduled for ten o'clock on a specific day. Initially this meeting had been scheduled for the week following, but had been rescheduled on Anna's request, bringing it forward by one week.

The meeting was to be as early as possible in the morning with the hope that she would be sober at that time. Anna had previously been informed that counseling could only proceed with her on the basis that she would be sober.

Accompanied by Casy, a counseling colleague, we arrived at Anna's residence at about ten o'clock. We found her radio playing quite loudly making it difficult for her to hear us knocking. I opened the door and stood in the foyer calling her. Anna came

walking towards us from the far end of the lounge with a blood-
ied towel wrapped around her wrists. My first thoughts were that
this may have been an act of self-harm.

There was fresh blood and glass from a broken bottle scat-
tered all over the kitchen floor. I grabbed Anna and held the towel
tight. I then asked Casy to dial 000 (the Australian emergency
telephone code) to request an ambulance. I heard a car stopping
outside the house; it was her pastor arriving for the meeting as
scheduled. I then cancelled the idea of calling 000.

After taking control of the situation, I confronted Anna. She
said that she had slipped and fallen when she handled a glass
bottle. That was when she had cut herself. She also had a cut
above the eye, which did not seem to have been more than skin
deep. Anna was highly intoxicated. I again asked her what happened. Anna said for a second time that she had slipped and fell.

Anna's pastor offered to drive her to the local hospital while
we followed. She was attended to at the emergency section. We
left about an hour later while her pastor stayed with her.

In speaking with Anna's pastor later that afternoon he reported
that she was clear about the accident—that she had slipped while
handling a bottle at the sink area in the kitchen. She also acknowledged and understood that working with her can only be beneficial when she is of sober mind. This was an approach shared by
both myself and her pastor.

Generating hypotheses in Anna's situation couldn't be done
without her life story as well as her past and present behavior. Her
ongoing drinking, increased level of alcohol abuse, and behavior of physical abuse to herself—often talking about suicide and
harming others played a major part when seeking ways and means
of counseling her.

Hoff (2001, 171) states that people often give clues and warnings about their intentions. When looking back at the progress of ninety-seven days without drinking and comparing it with her downward spiral into depression, it became difficult to accept that cutting her wrists was an accident. All information indicated towards a typical act of self-harm. However, I still have hope for her rehabilitation, as research shows that a great number of young people abusing alcohol end up changing to healthier lifestyles.

Anna often phoned me at home after hours to talk about daily happenings. Sometimes we spoke for long periods of time. Her pastor, whom I got to know well, continued to work with her after I moved out of the area. I remember him telling me how he was determined not to give up. Anna went on attending church services knowing that she was not being judged. She felt good about socializing in an environment where she experienced a sense of belonging. She engaged in psychiatric treatment while she was building social relationships among church groups. With continuous support Anna moved towards a positive lifestyle. These were positive signs and I believe she was on her way to recover from her drinking disease.

The case with Anna is an example of how difficult it can be to cure from alcohol abuse. The first step of working towards abstinence or reduced use was achieved for a short period. As small as it might seem it is an example that it can be achieved. Not giving up by both the client and the counselor is a critical factor in counseling. As a clinician once commented during a seminar on binge drinking among young people, "A breakthrough came after some thirteen years. What was real thirteen years ago did not appear to be real anymore."

Case Example Two: Caron

Caron, a fifty-eight-year-old married woman called from work requesting to meet with me. We arranged to meet at a coffee shop, which she suggested. Caron explained that she could not cope with her daughter Yvonne's drinking behavior anymore. Although Yvonne did not live with Caron in the same apartment, Caron felt anxious all the time. Her sleep was being disturbed with spells of waking up during the night sweating thereafter she couldn't fall asleep again. Going to work tired was not doing her well and she believed that her business was being compromised. Yvonne was drinking on the job. Employing her daughter made Caron feel good. However, she wanted to think that it may have exacerbated Yvonne's disrespectful, loud, and sometimes violent behavior. Yvonne was an office employee at her mother's business. Caron felt very angry about the situation because she loved her daughter. She couldn't understand why this was happening to her.

According to Caron, her daughter, now twenty-seven years old, started drinking when she was about twelve years old. Caron recalled that she did not condone Yvonne's teenage drinking. However, she did not approve of it with the belief that it was a teenage thing and that curiosity would come to pass. She noticed that two years later Yvonne started drinking regularly with friends and also occasionally smoked cannabis. Yvonne became very rebellious when spoken to by her mother about her drinking habits. She also became somewhat aggressive and abusive in her behavior. Until Yvonne turned nineteen, her life was arranged around her drinking sprees with friends. This impacted on her school performance to the extent that she once ran off with a boyfriend. Wanting to be a good mother and not wanting to escape her responsibilities as a parent, Caron continued to support Yvonne.

She supported her with rent for Yvonne's apartment, clothing, food, and daily needs, knowing that some of the same money was spent on alcohol. Caron also kept contact with Yvonne and showed appreciation when she visited. Yet Yvonne's abusive behavior towards her family did not stop. It actually increased to the extent when she once physically harmed Caron and Yvonne's sister when they would try to calm Yvonne down. Caron reported that this had been her life for the past fifteen years. She felt that she needed support in finding a solution.

Yvonne, in turn, blamed her mother for her drinking. Caron was not aware of any psychological or emotional history that could have caused her to do so. The only factor that might have had an influence could have been Caron's separating from Yvonne's father during her childhood days.

Caron remarried and her social life after work was seemingly arranged around her home and her new husband. They socialized during weekends when children and friends visited. There was no history of medical or psychiatric disorder associated with either Yvonne or any family member.

Caron had three children from her first marriage of whom Yvonne was the youngest. She had a close relationship with her oldest daughter who was very supportive to Caron in her anxious and stressful situation with Yvonne. Her son had moved out and was self-supportive and independent. Caron divorced from Yvonne's father during her childhood days and had subsequently remarried with no children from this marriage. Caron's new husband had three children from his previous marriage that lived independent from them. He supported Caron in her personal struggle with Yvonne's drinking problem and unacceptable behavior; however, he did not get involved in any disciplinary matters pertaining to Yvonne.

Caron was of the opinion that maybe she was too liberal in the bringing up of her children and especially in the case of Yvonne. She believed that allowing her children all the freedom of choice was the right thing to do. Her former husband and father of her three children had the same approach. Caron believed then that it was just the right thing to do; to give her children the opportunity to be who they felt they wanted to be and not to engrain the kind of discipline, boundaries, traditions, and rules she was brought up with. When she compared her children with one another, all being between twenty-seven and thirty-five years old, she could not understand why Yvonne seemed to have gone the route she had taken. Caron felt that she wanted to give them the best chance to discover themselves, to be themselves, and to search for their own individual identities. However, she believed that something about Yvonne's personality and rebellious behavior was overlooked or rather simply ignored.

According to Caron they had a fairly stable financial life. She remembered giving money for things that might not have been necessary only to get them satisfied and quiet. Giving them money was also one of those things Caron could and wanted to do. Money was one thing she did not have much of as a child.

Caron couldn't cope with her daughter's behavior when she was drinking. She lacked motivation to continue with life while she battled with sober cognitions.

Caron seemingly drew Yvonne's drinking problem towards herself and felt that she was responsible for Yvonne's behavior. Although her thoughts caused extreme internal conflict she believed that it was meant to be this way. Caron's constant mental preoccupation with the situation clouded any sober thoughts and this manifested in sleeplessness, stress, and anxiety. The more she tried to help, the less progress was made. She ended up being an angry person. Yvonne's drinking problem was getting worse rather than better.

As Caron was at a dead end with self-help efforts she quickly responded to counseling support. Follow-up sessions were focused on helping her to assert herself with identified goals. She quickly realized that she was not in control of Yvonne's life. She also distinguished the difference between control and influence. What Caron did pick up on was taking control of her own life. CBT, Solution-Focused and Strength-Based Therapy helped Caron to do some self-regulated exercises. She took control and cognitively diverted from being preoccupied with Yvonne's drinking behavior to positive self-talk.

It became evident that Caron relied on direct guidance, helping her towards set goals. She stated that she had made much progress, was sleeping better, and was not cognitively preoccupied with Yvonne anymore. She experienced less anxiety attacks and her decision-making was focused on taking control of interrelation situations with her daughter. Caron had also managed to divorce her role as employer from that of being a mother with the result that clear boundaries were being set in the work place. Caron reported of feeling much less angry about the whole situation and realized that she was not responsible for Yvonne's drinking and behavior. Further sessions followed as Caron relied on counseling support to further develop her asserting skills, stress management, and cognitive/behavioral control of the situation.

Once during a telephone session Caron reported that the progress she had made was somewhat unbelievable. Her voice sounded like someone speaking from a point of new departure, with renewed confidence and someone who was totally in control of their life again. She was precise and accurate, and she mentioned how she was so pleased that she did not sell her business as she had thought, with the purpose of running away from every-thing. Once she realized that she was in control of her life again, she maintained asserting herself in her relationship with Yvonne in a relationship she believes has never been better in the past fifteen years.

Caron's relationship had grown better in more than one way. The paradox in this story lies in the changing behavior of not only Caron but in the behavior of Yvonne as well. I was told that Yvonne had moved on from working for her mother to a job that she always wanted to do. She was earning a bigger salary and apparently enjoying the work more than what she did before. Yvonne continued visiting Caron and other family but without the old habit of taking any alcoholic drinks to her parents' place. What Caron appreciated the most was that Yvonne's life of secrets and lies about her substance use had shown signs of change. This, Caron believes, is a recipe for a great relationship, one that she was looking forward to.

References

Frances, R. J., J. Franklin, and K. Flavin. 1986. Suicide and alcoholism: *Annals of the New York Academy of Sciences* 487(1): 316–326.

Hoff, L. A. 2001. *People in crisis*, 5th ed. San Francisco: Jossy-Bass.

Perkinson, R. R. 2004. *Treating alcoholism: Helping your clients find the road to recovery.* New Jersey: Wiley.

Report on Substance Abuse in Australia. 2003. House of Representatives, Australian Parliament. Retrieved February 11, 2008 from http://www.apl.gov.au/house/committee.

Roesler, W. 1989. Alcoholism. *Clinical and Experimental Research* 13(4): 484.

Rogers, C. R. 1980. *A way of being.* Boston: Houghton Mifflin.

Wagner, C. C., and B. T. McMahon. 2004. *Rehabilitation Counseling Bulletin* 47 (3): 152–161.

WHO Global Status Report on Alcohol. 2004. Retrieved February 12, 2008 from http://www.who.int/substance_abuse/publications/en/australia.

Chapter Nine

Obesity

Recent years have seen an appropriate accentuation of interest in basic metabolic processes. There are many similarities between the problems involved in obesity, substance abuse and other addiction disorders. While many people have been confronted with the problem of obesity, the medical case for obesity prevention and management has never been stronger. Major efforts are now being taken to identify promising routes to address this problem.

Behavioral Similarities

Addictions and eating disorders, as mentioned, share many commonalities. While addiction has been defined as a disease characterized by the repetitive and destructive use of one or more mood-altering drugs, in an eating disorder it is a maladaptive pattern of binge-eating that leads to impairment or distress. The commonalities between obesity and other addictions entail three or more of the following:

- Tolerance
- Withdrawal
- The substance (food) was taken in larger amounts or over longer periods than was intended
- A great deal of time is spent in activities necessary to obtain the food
- Persistent desire or unsuccessful efforts to cut down or control use
- Important social, occupational or recreational activities are given up
- Continued eating with the knowledge of having a physical or psychological problem that was likely to have been caused or exacerbated by the substance (food)

The phenomenological similarities between obesity and other substance abuse disorders include:

- A higher than average family history of substance abuse and or obesity
- Cravings for food or a psychoactive substance
- Cognitive dysfunction
- The use of food to relieve negative effect (anxiety and depression)
- Secretiveness about the behavior
- Social isolation and maintenance of the problem behavior despite adverse consequences
- Denial of the presence and severity of the disorder
- Depression

Physical and Psychological Complications of Obesity

Obesity has many causes and may be divided into groups of which binge eating is one. Binge eating is perhaps the most common yet the least researched and is, like drug addiction, characterized by a pathological attachment. Binge eating includes obsessive thoughts about food and compulsion to eat more than most people would eat within similar periods and in similar circumstances. Like cocaine addiction or alcoholism, the binge eater cannot take or leave it—*they cannot eat just one.*

Diseases and Conditions Associated with Obesity

Associated metabolic consequences. Metabolic consequences of obesity are highly dependent on body fat distribution. Increased abdominal fat is associated with insulin resistance while it releases free fatty acids. This process ends in a negative response that in turn may result in many harmful conditions of which coronary heart disease, a variety of cancers, and type 2 diabetes are the most common.

Problems associated with excess weight.

- Skin complications
- Degenerative joint diseases
- Hernia
- Respiratory diseases
- Varicose veins
- Hemorrhoids
- Werner's syndrome

- Sleep apnea
- Oedema cellulites
- Stress incontinence
- Problems with self-esteem

Problems with well-being directly associated with obesity.

- Back pain
- Depression
- Social isolation
- Decreased libido
- Snoring
- Sleep deprivation
- Breathlessness
- Asthma
- Fatigue
- Impotence
- Sweat

Studies have shown a number of common reasons for being overweight such as:

- It is just too hard to lose it
- I need to eat to cope
- Being fat means I do not have to:
  - Be sexual
  - Go places and meet people
  - Compete with slimmer, prettier people
- Being fat is me being an individual; I do not want to be liked for my body
- I am warmer and cuddlier this way

Self-Control and Obesity

Research has found that greater maintenance of weight loss occurred when the therapist was *faded out* during treatment, resulting in the client fading out soon after. Although treatment varies considerably from study to study, the greater success regarding weight loss tends to be associated with longer treatment periods. It has been estimated that only 5 percent of all obese persons treated in short-term exercises will reach their ideal weight. However, physical exercise such as general housework and gardening, walking at a moderate rate for about twenty minutes per day, and playing some kind of physical sport have a positive impact.

Clients need to learn self-control rather than abstinence. Thus, a typical program with a weekly goal of a small amount of weight loss would be reasonable. It may also be useful to establish long-term goals. It is important to point out that treatment will focus on *behaviors* that lead to weight loss and ultimately to maintenance of a desired weight rather than on weight loss itself. The self-control approach, with its emphasis on small amounts in weight loss and psychological interventions that make eating behaviors relatively easy, is a rather painless approach to counter obesity (e.g., eating smaller portions than what are normally routine).

Weight Control Through Counseling in Groups

Probably the most unique aspect of counseling in groups rather than individuals, is the tenet that compulsive eaters can develop a natural, healthy relationship with food. Therefore, weight loss is neither a goal nor a measure of success. The behavior of routine exercise and changed eating habits become the goals while weight loss is merely a result. Their specific counseling goals are to explore individual's history with compulsive eating and body image issues, educate on some of the origins of women's food and body issues, lessen the negative impact of individual and societal messages regarding women's bodies, foster greater body acceptance, establish demand eating, improve self-esteem, and identify and begin to deal with possible issues underlying compulsive eating disorders. To overcome the social dynamics that lead to compulsive eating and body hatred, educating the community at large is a long-term goal.

References

Befort, C., M. F. Nicpon, S. E. Robinson-Kurpius, L. Huser, E. Hull-Blanks, and S. Sollenberger. 2001. Body image, self-esteem, and weight-related criticism from romantic partners. *Journal of College Student Development* 42: 407–419.

Corey, M. S., and G. Corey. 2006. *Groups: Process and practice, 7th ed.* Fullerton. California State University.

Donovan, D. M., and G. A. Marlatt. 1988. *Assessment of addictive behaviors.* New York: The Guilford Press.

Halford, W. K., and H. J. Markman, eds. 1997. *Clinical handbook of marriage and couples interventions.* Somerset: Bookcraft Ltd.

Hydock, R., and D. Eckstein. 2006. Help me help you: A systematic approach to goal support for couples. *The Family Journal—Counseling for Couples and Families.* April: 164–167.

Jacobson, N. S., and A. S. Gurman. 1986. *Clinical handbook of marital therapy.* New York: The Guilford Press.

Kowal, J., and S. M. Johnson. 2003. Chronic illness in couples: A case for emotionally focused therapy. *Journal of Marital and Family Therapy* 29(3): 299–310.

Lowinson, J. H., P. Ruiz, R. B. Millman, and J. G. Langrod. 2004. *Substance abuse: A comprehensive textbook,* 4th ed. Versailles: Quebecor World.

Masters, J. C., T. G. Burish, S. D. Hoolon, and D. C. Rimm. 1987. *Behavior therapy: Techniques and empirical findings,* 3rd ed. San Diego: Harcourt Brace Jovanovich.

Miller, D., and J. L. Brown. 2005. *Marital interactions in the process of dietary change for type 2 diabetes.* Pennsylvania: The University Press.

Mondanaro, J. 1989. *Chemically dependent woman: Assessment and treatment.* USA.

Chapter Ten

Understanding a Person in Crisis

Understanding a person in crisis is the cornerstone, or start-ing block, for crisis counseling. A good assessment, a good intervention plan, and proper follow-up derive from understand-ing the origin of crisis and how it relates to prediction, prevention, and resolution. Crisis counseling further demands understand-ing of how a crisis is related to illness and stress, how it devel-ops, and how different people resolve crises. Good information of how a problem started enhances our chances of dealing with crises better. Numerous factors that vary from person to person interact to produce a crisis, which is manifested in emotional, cognitive, and biophysical behaviors. Coping with stressful life events revolves around a relationship between stress and illness. In many instances this relationship results in people falling into a downward spiral, leading to a variety of psychological illness and sometimes suicide.

The following two case examples are stories of clients involved in crisis-counseling. Bray was diagnosed with HIV and AIDS and was experiencing rage and despair. Mary, on the other hand, overspent on her credit card. (Their real names are not used.) They were both counseled from a perspective of someone in a crisis. At the end of their respective counseling periods, both Bray and Mary were experiencing positive life change. Although their stories are radically different, the events they were exposed to both lead to an individual situation of crisis.

Case Example One: Bray

From a crisis counseling perspective and with specific attention to best practice and ethical issues, the work with Bray emphasizes his stressful life associated with the event when he visited his GP. During this visit Bray was diagnosed with AIDS. He was experiencing rage and despair, hence his desperate search for comfort.

Bray's urgency for counseling and his experience of shock required immediate attention. His added feelings of a life going "belly-up" required careful and critical assessment. It is crucial not to indulge in rescue fantasies. Hoff cautions that in the absence of sound theoretical base and established techniques, there is not much to distinguish crisis intervention from intuitive first aid. Inadequate assessment prior to helping is often responsible for lifelong destructive effects. A careful assessment is critical and that it is the first step in making an appropriate evaluation of the client's situation.

Further critical factors relating to the crisis assessment are described by Hoff (2001) in a seven-point model. Bureaucracies (administrative processes in hospitals, clinics, and similar institutions) often jeopardize the human aspect of crisis intervention. This prevents distressed people from receiving adequate help at a critical point. The next seven points contribute towards crisis intervention in the following ways:

1. The assessment process must be linked to crisis resolution.
2. The assessment must occur immediately.
3. The focus of the assessment is on identifiable problems rather than personality dynamics or presumed coping deficits.
4. Historical information is vital about the person in solving problems, resolving crises, and dealing with stressful life events.
5. The assessment is not complete without assessing risk of life.
6. A crisis assessment is not to a person but with a person. A service contract is therefore a logical outcome of appropriate crisis assessment.
7. Integral to a crisis assessment are cultural and community resources, as manifestations of crisis. They are often social and individual.

It is thus very important to do the crisis assessment before any attempt to commence treatment, as knowledge of the factors guides us in assessing what any treatment might be. Bray in his situation of rage, shock, and despair required careful immediate assessment. It helped to examine Bray's concepts of his crisis and lead to answers on questions I had relating to Bray's feelings and thoughts. Information about how his crisis-state developed and how it had manifested in his emotional behavior was priority. Creating an intervention plan is impossible without this information.

Being diagnosed with AIDS was certainly unexpected by Bray. It was unanticipated. He was overwhelmed with shock. He was unable to solve this problem in a usual manner as he had lost his strong sense of identity. Typically, he was one in crisis as he had suffered a sudden loss of his future and his comfort disappeared without warning.

Was Bray is in denial or did he accept the diagnosis? This was the question I needed answered, and I hoped to find it soon during the initial session. Once clarity had been determined about denial or acceptance, then I would be able to inform Bray of the facts to ensure that ignorance did not prevail. As sexual decision-making is a complex issue and not only a matter of *yes or no*, clear understanding was paramount. Among some AIDS patients, *free-floating* anger results in irresponsible sexual behavior with a risk of infecting others.

Although Bray survived an anti-gay bashing earlier in his life, the reality of the ferocity and violence connected to it was still an emotional and stressful experience to him, adding to his situation of suffering from AIDS. Bray's emotional state was in the context of having contracting AIDS and being victimized through anti-gay bashing. Although he experienced anti-gay bashing earlier in his life, it was the diagnosis of AIDS that prompted him to come for counseling.

He could easily have fallen into a downward spiral. Venting rage and anger inwards, and possibly outwards towards other people to end his pain, could have ended up in suicide. It could have prevented any chance of healing. It was therefore crucial for Bray to acknowledge the pain caused by the bashing and the news about the AIDS. But in the same time he had to keep in mind the fact that downward spiral is something he would experience and couldn't escape.

Bray's experience of rage and despair was a common emotional response to a traumatic life event. Anger did not arise simply from the misfortune of facing an untimely death but also from unfair violent treatment by a society with limited tolerance for someone who was perceived to be different. Furthermore, his anxiety went beyond his own personal misfortune. Bray was also anxious about other people involved in his present and past love affairs.

The assessment indicated that Bray's emotional status was linked to a need for counseling. The risk of him falling into a downward spiral was high. This could have increased his chances of ending up with a negative resolution, such as suicide or episodes of psychosis, only to have remained in crisis. Through effective crisis intervention it was possible to reduce Bray's vulnerability by increasing his coping ability. This was achieved by identifying other social support systems that already existed, such as his supportive circle of friends. He was also taking prescribed medicine to which he responded positively. Bray was tested by his own spiritual beliefs and requested a visit by a local pastor known to him. This matter was arranged with the same urgency during the first session.

Planning toward a positive resolution was of utmost importance to establish rapport with Bray. It was critical to know that both of us were congruent in factors pertaining to his crisis. If communication had failed and I had appeared shocked or critical Bray could have felt alone, abandoned, worthless, and hopeless. Making meaning of his circumstances, work status, social role, and sexuality, cultural values and privacy play pivotal roles in the outcome of the counseling process. This is endorsed by Kisthardt (2001, 174) in emphasizing that we must "be sensitive to cultural factors," and, "assist people in involvements that hold meaning for them."

While the most tragic result of failed communication is violence towards self and others, Bray did not show desire of revenge or to end his life. His emotional status typified a life crisis, which included ramifications such as the feeling of losing his future, and it should be noted that suicide among people with AIDS is common. Additional factors such as anti-gay violence, a fragile social network support, family and community crises, doubts of a future occupation, a radical life cycle transition, and the prognosis of death increase the risk of both suicide and homicide.

At thirty-four years old, Bray was at the peak of his life and the event of being diagnosed with such a fatal disease reversed for him the natural process of life-span development. This forced him to face death at a time in his life when he was at the peak of energy, independence, sexuality, and occupation. Also prevalent in Bray's situation was societal discrimination, which he already experienced through anti-gay bullying, an issue that he was still grappling with.

Although communication was important, without rapport there was no foundation for successful progress. A respectful approach reflected true concern for Bray's situation. My reflection of empathy, caring, and sincerity strengthened the relationship. Bray felt that he was understood and that all unclear issues had been addressed in a clear and simple way.

Although some may argue that in certain circumstances there is no time to plan as life-and-death issues may be at stake, a good plan can be formulated in a few minutes by someone who knows the signs of crisis. They need to be confident in their ability to help, and be able to enlist additional, immediate assistance in cases of impasse or life and death emergency. The time spent on a good plan can prevent injuries and save lives.

Bray's crisis-state demanded for a useful plan that consisted of all the specific intentions of the treatment. These intentions were directly connected to the information gained from the assessment and were necessary to address questions pertaining to the case. The following key questions were relevant in Bray's case. The following questions are important considerations behind the construction of a good intervention plan:

To what extent was Bray's normal life disrupted?
Was he able to perform his job?
Could Bray handle his daily responsibilities such as eating
  and personal hygiene?
Did his situation disrupt anyone else?
To what extent was he victimized by the anti-gay bullying?
Did Bray show signs of suicide, homicide or both?
How close was Bray to despair?
Was his perception of reality disrupted and if so, to what
  extent?
Was Bray's social support system informed and available?

Careful analysis of all the available information should help the counselor to construct an intervention plan that involves the client thinking through the events. It is important to know what a client thinks, what he or she feels, and how he or she behaves. This will help to formulate some possible solutions, with help from family or support group members, if necessary. The intervention plan can then be tested by asking which resolutions the client would prioritize as most urgent. By doing this the client will feel part of the solution as well as being part of making decisions pertaining to personal matters.

Setting goals for the immediate future is a basic element of the intervention plan. Decision counseling is cognitively oriented and may help to put any distorted thoughts, chaotic feelings and disturbed behavior into order while a client searches for solutions.

A client can also appraise the meaning of problems, i.e., how they feel about problems, why the problems are here, or what influence these problems will have on their life in the future. He or she can find ways to overcome the pain and the feeling of being belly-up. Knowledge of a client's functional capacity and their network of social attachments can be used effectively in the intervention plan. It will help in assessing coping abilities and problem-solving skills, which in turn may help in the decision counseling process.

After evaluating a client's crisis situation the counselor will confirm the intervention plan. The plan will be confirmation that the counselor and the client have mutually worked at the intervention plan, which should include:

- The client is in charge of his or her future
- He or she is able to make decisions
- The therapeutic relationship is between the client and the counselor
- Both parties have rights and responsibilities
- The relationship between counselor and client is on equal footing

Critically important to the plan is that only what has been agreed upon is included and each partner keeps a copy.

Effective crisis care is based on the contents of the agreed plan. It focuses on growth that avoids negative, destructive outcomes of traumatic events. This means working through the intervention plan in the context of the client's thinking, feeling, and behavior. Ineffective coping in any of these realms can be thought of as a red flag, signaling negative crisis outcomes. Such signals and signs indicate that help is needed and that crisis intervention strategies are to be actioned.

Because the sad news about AIDS became known to Bray at an unexpected time, his emotional experience of a lost future was very painful. Therefore his natural tendency was to avoid coming to terms with it immediately and directly, hence the rage and despair.

Understanding Bray's problem through carefully assessing his situation had directly supported the compilation of an intervention plan in collaboration with him. Working with him in an authentic manner had created a therapeutic relationship that helped Bray to disclose his thoughts and feelings. It also added to a relationship of trust. Through the therapeutic process Bray had been encouraged to examine the total problem; the diagnosis of AIDS and the anti-gay bashing, his own behavior, his emotional status, and physical responses. His thoughtful reflections on his life lead to growth and positive change rather than self-pity and self-depreciation.

He could easily have adopted a victim role or blamed others for his situation. As this is in many cases a possibility, the counseling process must make provision for guidance to the contrary. His survival skills were tapped for constructive crisis resolution. Encouragement channeled his rage and feeling of revenge into action to positive life change. This process of change coincided with his newly learned coping devices, while his successful problem solving mechanisms were reinforced.

Bray's supportive circle of friends was extremely useful as they were linked to the treatment plan. The resolution of Bray's crisis laid within one of the most powerful means of restoring him in a healthy way, namely his network of supportive friends. This perspective is supported by Maxmen and Ward (1995, 92). They write that during an acute psychosis "supportive psychotherapy is the verbal therapy; it provides reality testing, emotional comfort and help in distinguishing between sensible and senseless ideas, feelings and actions." The counselor takes an active role in reinforcing this natural resource, a technique known as *social network intervention.*

Historical data reveals that people suffering from AIDS do not want to be treated as victims. This was also the case with Bray. The counseling relationship and the endeavor to know and understand him strengthened the therapeutic relationship. This in turn allowed for critical factors to be identified and acted upon. Proper and comprehensive assessment helped us both to focus on the critical issues. Crucial information supported the identification of specific goals, which in turn helped to set up an intervention plan with positive resolution strategies. Working strictly in accordance with these strategies helped to turn Bray's shock, rage, and despair into positive change. Through follow-up sessions, the counseling treatment process supported him to get back to his normal self. Bray responded positively to the medication he was prescribed by his GP. After a couple of sessions with Bray and his employer, helping them to understand his condition, Bray continued in his occupation with renewed enthusiasm. Bray sold his house, which turned out to be too much for him to cope with. He lacked the energy that house chores and general maintenance demanded of him. Bray then moved in with friends where he felt supported and valued. I still remember something he said to me during our last session as he was about to leave the room. He turned around, looked me in the eyes, smiled and said, "It is so satisfying to be in a non-judgmental environment, I like my job and my friends."

Case Example Two: Mary

The following transcript reflects Mary's position. The counseling session was taped on video for the purpose of keeping the transcript as original as possible. Mary was shocked by the news from her bank manager that she had overspent her credit card, with result that she might lose her property. The news left her feeling overwhelmed, her mind clouded and her thinking disrupted. Mary's story, as in Bray's, is a typical situation of someone in a crisis.

Mary entered the counseling room not looking at me while she was leaning her chin in her left hand. She stood quietly for a while before she responded to my invitation to have a seat. I also did not speak at that moment and allowed her to initiate any talk when she was feeling ready to do so. I had earlier that day arranged her appointment when she phoned.

MARY: Hi James, how are you?

JAMES: I'm well thank you; you don't seem to be that well today.

MARY: No, I am not too good at the moment, a bit, a bit stressed out.

JAMES: A bit stressed, about what?

MARY: Mmm, (sits silent for a while). I got a phone call from the bank manager today, and it appears that I am overdrawn by a lot of money, and I just don't get how I got there. Yeah, it just all suddenly happened, and I am like, oh my God, how am I going to get out of this? Yeah, can't even think straight, ah, yeah, not good.

JAMES: What is your thinking on this? How are you going to get out of this?

MARY: I, ah, I don't know, like I don't have any more money. The credit card debt's up, there is no buffer there, there is no one to phone. I don't have my family; I can't get them to help. I can't work any harder than I am. You know, I am already doing full-time work, and I can't get any extra hours. I am quite, sort of overwhelmed. I don't think that I can pay for your session today. It is just, I don't know, I have no one to call.

JAMES: I can see that it is all getting to you. How is it getting to you?

MARY: I am scared that, that I am just not going to have any money, and I will lose the house and I'm going to lose my job and I am just going to get so stressed. Yeah, it's just, yeah. I don't know how I am going to get out of this.

JAMES: Well maybe you can tell me how you got into it?

MARY: Mmm, I am not really sure, like, ah, I think, you would think that I was obviously living beyond my means is how I got into it. But I never learned how to live within my means. I never learned how to budget, and I thought that I was budgeting really well. And then I got sick, and I had to go into surgery, and that cost me three grand, and that got put onto the credit card, and the next minute I am getting phone calls from people saying I am not paying my bills. I hate that feeling. I hate owing people money and not being responsible for my own wellbeing.

JAMES: Ok, have you spoken to someone else about it since this morning, since you learned about it from the bank manager?

MARY: No, I have just basically been going through my finances over and over and over again, trying to see what I can do, and I just get really more upset. I just feel that I make the same mistakes that my family made, and that is how they value life, just going through one pay-packet to the next and being in debt all their life. They are still in debt and in their sixties, and that thought, ending up like them, is an extra weight onto the issue.

JAMES: So how do they cope?

MARY: Well the way they get out of debt is they accidentally win money, and they pay their debt. In a year's time their back in the position they were in when they paid it off. Or someone dies. Like grandma died and they got some. But they don't support me, and there is no way they are going to give me money. They have none, and they will just blame me for my stupidity in doing it.

JAMES: Your mortgage, is it at the same bank where your credit card is, or does another financial institution hold the mortgage?

MARY: At the same bank.

JAMES: Mmm (short silent moment). How do you feel now sitting here talking about it?

MARY: (At this moment she changed her sitting position, and the expressions on her face were reflecting less concern.) Better than I did this morning when I was feeling alone, sort of didn't know what to do.

JAMES: Well, that is a good sign, isn't it, Mary?

MARY: Yeah, I just hate being like this. I just hate the situation being like this, being co-dependent. Mmm, still feeling isolated and frightened for what is going to happen to me.

JAMES: Do you have other supportive friends at work maybe or close friends?

MARY: Yip, I've got a few good friends, but I don't want to ask them for money, don't want to burden them with my difficulties.

JAMES: Any other support that you might be able to get, apart from financial support?

MARY: Well, I suppose they could give me some ideas. Like Dall and his brother; old friends of mine. They have been in trouble financially, well, actually, only recently. They might have some ideas in how to handle it and who to speak to. Dall's brother is a bank manager, quite high up at the bank that I am with, and he might be able to help me with some suggestions.

JAMES: Have you had any similar problems in the past?

MARY: Yeah, I have but not to this extent. All of it has eventually sorted itself out, and I got over it. What p...s me off so much is that I have gone and done it again.

JAMES: So it is not the first time?

MARY: (Somewhat uncomfortable in her posture and also searching for words) Yeah, ah [expletive] how many more times am I going to allow myself to get into this situation? So this seems to be a lesson I have to learn.

JAMES: Now let's go back to the first time. How did you cope with it then?

MARY: Well, that was when my grandma was still alive, so she helped me out. She gave me some money and got me through that. (A smile appears on Mary's face, and she is now also much more relaxed.)

JAMES: Well, nice to see you're smiling. What other options do you think you have, apart from going to your family or direct support groups or financial institutions?

MARY: Maybe talking with the bank and coming up with a solution.

JAMES: Did you have a problem with this specific bank before?

MARY: No, I never actually had (pauses for a short while). I don't have bad credit as I always got out of it myself before until when the bank came knocking at my door. So then I became aware of my past. Do you know what I mean?

JAMES: You are really helping me to understand what you mean, Mary. And I am getting the picture.

MARY: So maybe I should make an appointment and see what they think, and maybe we can sort the problem out. It's just about my privacy and my past.

JAMES: It sounds like a possibility. Would you be interested to learn some money-management skills?

MARY: Yeah. It's embarrassing though.

JAMES: It could be, but at the same time it could be a solution, couldn't it?

MARY: Yeah sure, sure.

JAMES: Just to recap. Apart from your financial issues now have you had any negative connotations to your bank in the past?

MARY: No, not at all. I have always paid everything on time.

JAMES: Well, Mary, you have more than one option. One, you

can go to the bank manager; two, you can go to Dall; three, you can get someone to share the unit; and four, you can have a garage sale. I think those are good ideas. It is question of prioritizing and deciding which one first. If you would put those options on the table now, which one would you opt for first?

MARY: I feel comfortable with going to Dall first. Getting ideas as to how to present a package and then go and talk to the bank manager. (She is acting normally and seems to be much more at ease.)

JAMES: Depending on the advice Dall gives you, you are going to the see the bank manager. Let's just go over the issue of renting out your flat again. Could it help you financially?

MARY: Probably, some hundred dollars a week extra money coming in while I cannot make extra money at work. It is just a matter of getting someone in quickly. That's the issue with the bank. It's like the bank at this point wants their money back like yesterday.

JAMES: Then there is the last one, and you said it yourself a few minutes earlier. That is not to get into financial debt again.

MARY: Mmm (pauses for a while, and there is absolute quiet for a long time).

JAMES: Can we talk about that idea, Mary? Do you mind? What solutions do you think there are?

MARY: To come up with a budget that works, that's functional, and to get rid of the credit cards so I don't have them. Because obviously it's not a fault, it's just one of those behaviors that works for the bank rather than for me. So it's best to get rid of them.

JAMES: It's basically like you taking control of it again?

MARY: Mmm (now seems happier).

JAMES: To summarize, can we just go over your options again? We have Dall and his brother's support because of their financial knowledge, we've got the bank, and you can share your flat. The first one is to go and see Dall and see if he can support you in this, help you to budget and see if he can help you with regard to your approach of the bank. The second one, then, is to make an appointment with the bank and see if they've got a solution. That's the second option. It all sounds good to me, it really does. Apart from that, I will suggest that we have a follow-up meeting. You're comfortable with that?

MARY: Yeah.

Mary's crisis situation that originated on the morning of the day of counseling was due to a telephone call from the bank manager. Mary was informed that she had overdrawn on her bank account, which resulted in the bank demanding immediate settlement on her overdraft or the repossession of her flat. At that moment Mary became overwhelmed with feeling alone, as she believed that she had no one to turn to and that she was going to lose her flat. She was also extremely concerned about her work and what the response of her employer would be. Although her personal behavior of overdrawing on her bank account was not the primary cause for her feeling overwhelmed, the thought of losing her flat and her job was creating the crisis. The factors placing people at risk vary and interact to produce a crisis that is manifested in emotional, cognitive, behavioral, and biophysical responses to traumatic life events. While Raphael et al. (2001) add personal characteristics as other factors that may have contributed to the ways that Mary reacted and dealt with the situation, Servaty-Seib (2004,133) writes that "reality is not objectively knowable." Therefore Mary's reactions may have been her subjective reconstruction of reality.

It was important to identify the origin of the crisis as it held a direct link to the development of Mary's crisis. She had in less than one day gone through the crisis development phases namely, the initial rise in her anxiety, her own inability to solve the problem, an increase in anxiety levels, and the remaining problem.

The thought of losing her flat and probably her job was a personal value that influenced the development of her subjective world. Also critically important to her was the issue of financial security and the foundation she needed to secure this. The *timing* of the event was not in her favor. She believed that her support elements at that moment were non-existent, that she had no one to turn to for help and that losing her flat would spiral her into *loneliness*. People generally operate on the basis of important assumptions and that stressful events may challenge these assumptions, which in Mary's case, have led to her feeling lonely and empty.

Working with Mary helped her to feel safe and secure. From a crisis counseling point of view it was as important to determine whether Mary had previously been exposed to traumatic events as it was to determine her current cognitive ability to resolve her crisis successfully. It was furthermore critical to determine whether her social support network was, as she believed, nonexistent, or if one did exist that could be used as an immediate basis for support. These factors hold the key that contribute to a favorable outcome of a crisis. From this point onwards we identified that she did in fact have someone that she could consult for financial advice and that she had an existing communication network that we could *immediately* pursue. Identifying this social support base was the turning point in Mary's emotional status and she *expressed a feeling of hopefulness.* Engaging the support of friends and social networks increases the likelihood for positive change.

Mary's body language and change of tone in her voice were signs that she was comfortable with the counseling relationship, which allowed for further exploration of her situation. Mary then admitted that she was previously involved in a similar financial situation when her grandma came to the rescue and she realized her responsibility in taking control of her finances. The stage was set to make Mary feel safe and secure. This atmosphere was necessary before taking the next step in allowing for an emotional arena. Allowing Mary to express her feelings about her crisis experience helped to begin the process of exploring the roots of her troublesome situation.

Mary's personal and immediate search for the cause of her crisis situation indicated a degree of urgency. It indicated signs of her personal strengths and her willingness to work towards a solution. Clients *need have a willingness to change* and examine themselves as Mary did, searching for meaning in the cause of her crisis.

Throughout the counseling session Mary acknowledged that she was responsible for overdrawing on her bank account. She first realized it when her grandma rescued her from debt. Acknowledging is one necessary part of building towards motivation to change her money-spending behavior. The other important part was when Mary indicated that she understood the importance and need of proper financial management.

Mary's participation in finding solutions was clearly visible throughout the counseling session. She was also aware that the possibility of losing her flat and probably her job was due to her behavior. Mary also understood that there was no one else to help her out as her grandma had and that she, in the counseling relationship, had to adopt a strategy, which could have a positive outcome.

During the counseling session Mary was guided through careful planning to gain new direction. After realizing that she had an existing social support system that may help her, Mary considered all actions that were possible to take. There is no substitute for a *good plan* for crisis resolution. The therapeutic alliance that was created with Mary, through interpersonal warmth, understanding, and continuous encouragement, allowed her to participate in prioritizing the identified options. It helped her to feel comfortable in the interview. Decision counseling is cognitive oriented and allowed Mary to put aside all distorted thoughts and feelings into some kind of order as she was encouraged to search for resolutions of the problem. What happens in a counseling room does not always conform to textbook perfection. The interaction between Mary and myself demonstrates exactly that. However, getting to understand Mary helped us both work towards a resolution that satisfied her. She knew that she was moving forward.

Ethical Issues

Throughout the interview, Mary reflected the sensitivity of her position. She was sharing personal issues about her current and private life, her past, and her friends. These matters are all confidential and have not only ethical but in some cases, legal boundaries.

Crisis is not emotional or mental illness, but it is a turning point in the life of someone that presents both danger and opportunity. It is an acute emotional upset arising from situational, developmental, or socio-cultural sources resulting in a temporary inability to cope by one's usual problem-solving devices.

What helped the therapeutic process towards a positive resolution was the step by step approach in terms of a plan. Following the intervention plan throughout the process supported Mary in solving her problem by instilling hope, changing her emotional state, identifying her social support network, identifying her options, and prioritizing them in a way that they strengthened her situation to the point of a positive outcome.

During a follow-up appointment Mary informed me that she retained her property. She was accompanied by her friend Dall during negotiations with the bank. Dall also helped her with ways to manage her finances better. Mary confessed that cutting up her credit card was hard to do. However, she did it and is now learning to live within her earnings.

References

Graham, H. L. 2004. *Cognitive-behavioral integrated treatment.* West Sussex: John Wiley and Sons, Ltd.

Hoff, L. A. 2001. *People in crisis,* 5th ed. San Francisco: Jossy-Bass.

Ivey, A. E., and M. B. Ivey. 2003. *Intentional interviewing and counseling.* USA: Phoenix Color Corporation.

Janoff-Bulman, R. 1989. Assumptive worlds and the stress of traumatic events: Application of the schema construct. *Social Cognition* 7(2).

Kisthardt, W. E. 2001. The strengths perspective in interpersonal helping. In *The strengths perspective in social work practice.* Boston: Allyn and Bacon.

Maxmen, J. S., and N. G. Ward. 1995. *Essential psychopathology and its treatment,* 2nd ed. New York: W. W. Norton and Company.

McBride, M. T. 2002. *Risky practices: A counselor's guide to risk management in private practice,* 2nd ed. Palmyra: Artproof Printing Company Pty Ltd.

McLeod, J. 2003. *An introduction to counseling.* Maidenhead: Open University Press.

Nelson. M. L. 2002. An assessment-based model for counseling strategy selection. *Journal of Consulting and Development* 80.

Raphael, B., C. Minkov, and M. Dobson. 2001. Psychotherapeutic and pharmacological intervention for bereaved persons. In *Handbook of bereavement research: consequences, coping and care.* Washington, DC: American Psychological Association.

Servaty-Seib, H. L. 2004. Connections between counseling theories and current theories of grief and mourning. *Journal of Mental Health Counseling* 26(2): 133.

Chapter Eleven

Psychosocial-Education and Dementia

Psychosocial-Education is helpful in providing support, training, and guidance to both people with organic and mental
illnesses and their families or caregivers. Studies tell us that psychosocial-education can help clients keep their moods more stable, stay out of the hospital, and generally function better. To help
the reader better understand the value of psychosocial-education
I focus on *dementia* as one type of mental illness rather than on
a variety. The focus is on the caregivers of people suffering from
dementia.

Personal and professional caregivers are regularly challenged
by behavior problems displayed by older adults with dementia.
Interference with effective communication results in decreasing
quality of life, which makes caring more difficult for caregivers.
Studies report that as many as 50 to 90 percent of individuals
with moderate and severe symptoms of dementia display clini-
cally significant behavior problems during the course of their
illness. Such problems and the difficulties they engender for
professional and personal caregivers demand comprehensive

interventions that incorporate professional development while systemic components in the provision of care also require ongoing development.

Behavioral excesses and deficits may be noted in functional and social domains of people with dementia, which may result in increased burden and stress on caregivers. Psychosocial-Education addresses teaching behavior management skills to caregivers plus a motivational system for maintaining the performance of these skills over the long-term.

Dementia as a Progressive Illness

Both vascular dementia and Alzheimer's disease are progressive illnesses and are common causes leading to functional complications, debilitation, and eventually death. Research shows a serious and common complication of dementia is the occurrence of mental and behavioral disturbances which manifest problematic behaviors. The resulting categories from 1,002 participants included delusions, hallucinations, agitation, depression, anxiety, elation, apathy, disinhibition, irritability, wandering, and pacing. Further results showed that participants with dementia were older, most often women, and less educated. The most frequent disturbance reported was apathy (27 percent). Depression and agitation or aggression were nearly as common, each reported in the 24 percent range.

These disturbances are associated with demanding personal care with worse prognosis, greater costs and increased caregiver burden, stress and professional caregiver turnover. In U.S. nursing homes the prevalence of behavior problems among persons with dementia ranges between 64 percent and 83 percent. Designing and developing effective interventions for management of behavior problems has become, as Allen-Burge et al. (1999, 213) describe, "a global health care concern."

Integrative Psychosocial-Educational Program

The ability to manage people with dementia and maximize quality of life can be enhanced if the appropriate information and support is available to caregivers, families, and communities. Caregivers play a vital role in providing direct care for people with dementia. Caregivers who are required to relinquish wage-earning positions in order to become caregivers (for example, a daughter to care for a parent) also face financial hardship, which adds to their stress. Absence of caregivers or stress among caregivers is a major predictor of early admission to residential care. However, despite this, many caregivers also report a sense of satisfaction with their work and a sense of accomplishment in keeping their relatives at home. A support program for caregivers, assisting them with management of behavioral problems and intermittent illness and facilitating referral to appropriate services when necessary, has been shown to delay admission of people with dementia to residential care. Studies to determine the effect of a structured intervention on caregivers of patients with dementia showed that some structured educational interventions help families deal with behavioral disorders, which reduces caregiver stress; and poor caregiver training was the most significant factor predicting nursing home placement, ahead of dementia severity, cognitive decline, and caregiver psychologic morbidity.

An Integrative Intervention Program

A specific training program presented by Burgio et al. (2001) includes a detailed staff training and performance feedback system for use in nursing homes. This program seeks to motivate staff to engage in behavioral interventions with people with dementia for the reduction of behavior problems. Specific behavioral skills, in-service training, and on-the-job training are included. The performance feedback system includes:

1. Enhanced job descriptions for nursing assistants (NA)
2. NA self-monitoring of performance
3. Management monitoring and feedback
4. Incentives
5. Written performance feedback

A further five-hour in-service training program covering five major skill areas is provided (Stevens et al. 1998):

1. Identifying environmental antecedents to resident problem behaviors
2. Communication skills training
3. Identifying the ABCs' of resident behaviors
4. Training in positive reinforcement procedures
5. Training in distraction and diversion techniques

Preliminary results indicated that nursing assistants offered more verbal prompts and activity announcements to residents after in-service and hands-on training. Communication skills, provision of physical assistance, and the use of distracting and diverting techniques were also improved. However, only units implementing continuous management by supervisory staff maintained NA performance gains over time; up to forty-six weeks post-training before training refreshment is required.

Management Factors

An additional forty-eight studies showed that due to a lack of follow-up evaluation by management or supervisory staff, the knowledge gained from training programs is not sustained in the long-term. Most studies do not consider organizational and system factors when planning and implementing training initiatives. This may account for difficulties encountered in the sustained transfer of knowledge to practice. Research found that management support was identified as the most important factor impacting the effectiveness of continuing training. Other factors included resources (staff, funding, and space) and the need for ongoing expert support.

Training and Support vs. Neuroleptics (Medication)

Studies were done in twelve nursing homes in London, Newcastle, and Oxford to evaluate the effectiveness of a training and support intervention program for nursing home staff. The outcome showed a reduction in the proportion of residents with dementia who have been prescribed neuroleptics (medication). Training and support intervention as alternatives to drugs was delivered to staff over a period of twelve months with the following results: residents taking neuroleptics in *alternative intervention* homes was 23 percent lower than those in controlled homes. The average reduction in neuroleptics use was 19.1 percent overall.

It was thus found that promotion of person-centered care and good practice in the management of persons with dementia provided an effective alternative to neuroleptics. Increasing knowledge, skills, and empathy significantly improved a caregiver's abilities in care-giving services. In addition, direct-care workers and employers rated the training highly and identified ways in which the course helped increase workers competence, empathy towards elder employees as well as patients, and self-esteem. This evidence challenges commonly held beliefs that no therapeutic intervention is of any value.

Needs Assessment

Over recent years there has been growing dissatisfaction about the quality of needs assessment services in New Zealand. Concern has been expressed that the model of needs assessment has major limitations, particularly for dementia, and that the assessment tools in use have not been validated. The quality of the assessment process is crucial for ensuring that people access appropriate services matched to their needs. For example, need for care is not solely determined by cognitive impairment but more by functional capacity and social support availability. Assessment services must ensure that there are safe and independent opportunities for people with dementia and their caregivers to provide feedback on the quality of these assessments.

A very important component of needs assessment and one that is often overlooked, is the burden placed on caregivers. There can be rewards as well as burdens in caring, but it is the burdens for which services must plan. Support for caregivers who wish to continue is essential. Over time the burden of caring can become too great even for the most committed caregiver. Many dementia sufferers ultimately require professional provision of twenty-four-hour care, which could result in high staff turnover. Research found that low staff turnover and high staff turnover were not associated with the same factors.

Assessment of Caregivers

All counseling begins with a process of assessment, which in many cases is separate from actual counseling. In some practices assessment is carried out by someone other than the counselor with the purpose of determining whether the person, or group, would benefit from counseling intervention. Standardized psychological tests can be used to evaluate a wide range of psychological and behavioral variables including social support and interpersonal functioning. Also available are open-ended questionnaires that people can complete in advance of the actual assessment interview. In the case of caregivers there are *caregiver burden scales* (available at counseling practices) that were designed to determine factors such as emotional effect, perceived change in living patterns, and relationships as a result of care giving.

Communication and Social Interaction

Social interaction requires additional important knowledge for the caregiver that includes a general familiarity with the distinctive social milieu of people with dementia. In the United States, this social context includes specific environments such as age-segregated housing, age-segregated social and recreational centers, the aging services network and age-segregated long-term care, as well as specific rules. An understanding of social context is thus based on both knowledge of what is supposed to be happening and the actual experience in operational institutions. Caregivers need to go beyond the commonly believed assumptions that living in an age-segregated environment will lead to increased friendships; this is somewhat naïve. In fact, many age-segregated environments are very intolerant of frailty and of social deviance of any sort.

The following two aspects are referred to as examples of how important it is for caregivers to understand the internal and external world of people with dementia:

First example: The functions of social interaction are numerous and diverse. From social interaction, people derive information and assistance from others, learn about their culture and history, and identify and select mates. At a more psychological level, social interaction is used to acquire and maintain self-identity, and does not occur without cost. Social interaction and maintenance of self-identity also require energy expenditure and risk the experience of negative emotions and threats of self-concept. Carstensen writes that individuals move through life with a group of people from whom they derive support, self-definition, and a sense of stability and continuity.

Second example: Improving communication is an attempt to increase the frequency of social interaction or to improve the quality thereof. *Behavioral* therapeutic interventions can be *individual-focused* through stimulus control, reminiscence, or spaced retrieval. *Environmental* based interventions, on the other hand, are focused on issues such as rearranging furniture, providing snacks in social areas, and fertilizing the surroundings with socially stimulating prosthetic memory aides. Individual and small-sample intervention studies have shown that external cues, coupled with minimal resident training, can increase residents' ward orientation and increase room finding. Further studies suggest the use of several types of external memory aids for dementia patients in order to increase social interaction, decrease passivity, and improve individual functioning. Aids include the use of notebooks, calendars, signs, and timers. Using prosthetic memory aids indicate that even severely demented people can increase the accuracy of what they say by using memory books with both familiar and novel social partners.

Competence

There are positive effects for residents, caregivers, and staff through participation in activities such as providing stimulation as well as relaxation. Music therapy, art, drama, dance, use of pets, and religious activities all add to a relaxed yet stimulated environment. Improvements in general orientation, independent functioning, and the use of initiative have been noted. Ongoing training of staff will contribute to the delivery of quality services incorporating the understanding and the value of such activities. Both on-the-job and formal educational programs are, according to Lewis, essential to maintain competence in the care of people with dementia. The training and development of caregivers working with people with dementia, in different settings and at different levels, is vital to ensure high quality care. Complaints about quality of care generally relate to staff that do not have an appropriate level of knowledge and understanding of dementia. A good understanding of dementia by caregivers at all levels will assist in better facility management and lessen breakdown in relationships, interaction, and communication.

Conclusion

On the one hand there is evidence that only specific types of care-giver and residential care staff education appears to have lasting effectiveness for the management of dementia-associated neuro-psychiatric symptoms. On the other hand there is also widespread failure to measure the level at which psychosocial treatment was implemented as intended, which would threaten internal and external validity and reliability. However, investigation and description of treatment process variables allows researchers to understand which aspects of the intervention are responsible for therapeutic change, potentially resulting in the development of more efficacious interventions. The development of quality indicators for use in measuring care outcomes remains an issue for future research.

To move towards a genuinely communicative, interpersonal model of care will require a more active partnership role for caregivers in the assessment and planning of services and a more co-operative working relationship among agencies. It will be important to know more about existing relationships among health professionals, family caregivers, and people with dementia. Studies suggest that having partnership in care giving appears to be an effective way to improve family-staff relationships in nursing homes.

In summary, studies in management culture in relation to the attainment of high quality care for people with dementia show that the establishment and maintenance of a person-centered approach of care within a supportive and innovative management culture is critical for positive outcomes. Burgio et al. (2003), however, goes one step further by suggesting that attention should be paid to the possible differential responses to interventions when race or differences in culture are involved between caregiver and care recipient.

Finally, taking into account all psychological and social factors of both the caregiver and the person with dementia, organizational and management support were identified as the most important factors impacting the effectiveness of continuing education as a psychosocial intervention program for caregivers of people with dementia.

References

Alessandro, N., R. Emma, T. Mauro, L. Ugo, M. Liscio, P. Bianca, and G. Salvini. 2004. The effect of a structured intervention on caregivers of patients with dementia and problem behaviors. *Lippincott Williams and Associated Disorders, Inc.* 18(2): 75–82.

Allen-Burge, R., A. B. Stevens, and L. D. Burgio. 1999. Effective behavioral interventions for decreasing dementia-related challenging behavior in nursing homes. *International Journal of Geriatric Psychiatry* 14: 213–232.

Aylward, S., P. Stolee, N. Keat, and V. Johncox. 2003. Effectiveness of continuing education in long-term care: A literature review. *The Gerontologist* 43: 259–271.

Bourgeois, M. S. 1991. Communication treatment for adults with dementia. *J. Speech Hearing Res.* 34: 831–844.

Brannon, D., J. S. Zinn, V. Mor, and J. Davis. 2002. An exploration of job, organizational, and environmental factors associated with high and low nursing assistant turnover. *The Gerontologist* 42: 159–168.

Braun, K. L., M. Cheang, and D. Shigeta. 2005. Increasing knowledge, skills, and empathy among direct care workers in elder care: A preliminary study of an active-learning model. *The Gerontologist* 45: 118–124.

Burgio, L., M. Corcoran, K. L. Lichstein, L. Nichols, S. Czaja, D. Gallagher-Thompson, M. Bourgeois, A. Stevens, M. Ory, and R. Schultz, 2001. Judging outcomes in psychosocial interventions for dementia caregivers: The problem of treatment implementation. *The Gerontologist* 41: 481–489.

————, A. Stevens, D. Guy, D. L. Roth, and W. E. Haley. 2003. Impact of two psychosocial interventions on white and African-American family caregivers of individuals with dementia. *The Gerontologist* 43: 568–579.

Camp, C. J., J. W. Foss, A. B. Stevens, C. C. Reichard, L. A. McKitrick, and A. M. O'Hanlon. 1993. Memory training in normal and demented elderly populations: The E-I-E-I-O model. *Exp. Aging Res.* 19: 277–290.

Carstensen, L. L. 1992. Social and emotional patterns in adulthood: Support for socio-emotional selective theory. *Psychology and Aging* 7(3): 331–338.

Fossey, J., C. Ballard, E. Juszczak, N. Alder, R. Jacoby, and R. Howard. 2006. Effect of enhanced psychosocial care on antipsychotic use in nursing home residents with severe dementia. *BMJ* 332: 756–761.

Hanley, I. G., and K. Lusty. 1984. Memory aids in reality orientation: A single-case study. *Behav. Res. Ther.* 22: 709–712.

Knight, B. G., and D. D. Satre. 1999. Cognitive behavioral psychotherapy with older adults. *Clinical Psychology: Science and Practice* 6(2): 188–203.

Lewis, H. 2002. Dementia in New Zealand: Improving quality in residential care. *Report to the Disability Issues Directorate.* New Zealand Ministry of Health.

Livingston, G., K. Johnston, C. Katona, J. Paton, and C. G. Lyketsos. 2005. Systematic review of psychological approaches to the management of neuropsychiatric symptoms of dementia. *American Journal of Psychiatry* 162: 1996–2021.

Lyketsos, C. G., M. Steinberg, J. Tschanz, M. C. Norton, D. C. Steffens, and J. C. S. Breitner. 2000. Mental and behavioral disturbances in dementia: Findings from the cache county study on memory in aging. *American Journal of Psychiatry* 157(5): 708–714.

McLeod, J. 2003. *An introduction to counseling*. Maidenhead: Open University Press.

Pillemer, K., J. J. Suitor, C. R. Henderson, R. Meador, L. Schultz, J. Robinson, and C. Hegeman. 2003. A cooperative communication intervention for nursing home staff and family members of residents. *The Gerontologist* 43: 96–106.

Rosen, J., L. Burgio, M. Kollar, M. Cain, M. Allison, M. Fogleman, M. Michael, and G. S. Zubenko. 1994. The Pittsburgh Agitation Scale: A user friendly instrument for rating agitation in dementia patients. *American Journal for Geriatric Psychiatry* 2: 52–59.

Stevens, A., L. D. Burgio, E. Bailey, K. L. Burgio, P. Paul, E. Capilouto, P. Nicovich, and G. Hale. 1998. Teaching and maintaining behavior management skills with nursing assistants in a nursing home. *The Gerontologist* 38: 379.

Stolee, P., J. Esbaugh, S. Aylward, T. Cathers, D. P. Harvey, L. M. Hillier, N. Keat, and J. W. Feighter. 2005. Factors associated with the effectiveness of continuing education in long-term care. *The Gerontologist* 45: 399–409.

Zimmer, J. G., N. G. Watson, and A. Treat. 1984. Behavioral problems among patients in skilled nursing facilities. *American Journal of Public Health* 76: 1118–1121.

Chapter Twelve

Culture in Counseling

Culture has some prominence in counseling. Our identity is a reflection of our culture, at least in its broader sense. Nationality, place or country of birth, religion, ethnicity, generational experiences, geographical location (urban or rural), sexual orientation, health, sport, and gender all contribute towards one's culture. From this point of view one already gets a sense of complexity when looking at multicultural societies. As travel has become safe, easy, and quick some people live in one country while traveling daily to work in another. Palmer and Laungani (1998) write that the world has turned into a global village. The New Zealand Ministry of Agriculture and Forestry reported in their rural bulletin in June 2002 that immigration from China and South Africa into New Zealand has increased 100 and 130 percent, respectively, since 1996. Forty-six percent of Australia's population was born overseas.

As in all other counseling matters, counselors must be aware of their own values and intentions. Counselors need to acknowledge cultural differences among clients while they remain conscious of the client's perspective. The same skills applied by counselors may have a different effect on people with varying cultural backgrounds. Diversity and different life experience will always stand out in the mainstream of counseling. The counselor, with every new session, looks at what the client brings with them. Such is the story of Sarah.

Case Example: Sarah

Sarah was a thirty-four-year-old single Venezuelan woman. At the time that she came for counseling, Sarah had been living in Australia for about twenty months. Although Sarah spoke Spanish at home, she did not require an interpreter to communicate in English. Being enthusiastic and keen to improve her English, Sarah tended to talk non-stop in a relatively loud tone, which could have been interpreted as being directive. She was a mestizo (of mixed Native American and European blood), and came from Caracas, which is the capital of Venezuela. Her religion was Roman Catholicism. When socializing, Sarah stood very close to others and maintained eye contact while chatting. Sarah had separated from her partner, who was an Australian. Her separation and her loneliness caused her to be anxious about making Australia her permanent home.

Sarah was culturally different. Her language, age, cultural background, religion, socio-economic background and socio-political ideals were different from mine. As I was aware about this difference, it was important to work with her by acknowledging her cultural background.

Constructing a Schematic Model

Many argue that our identity is shaped by influences that derive from particular membership that we have of a specific culture or cultures, that we reflect behaviors in our understanding of *good life.* Counseling people within the framework of multiculturalism compliments behaviorism, psychoanalysis, and humanistic psychology. According to McLeod (2003) this approach, acknowledging culture, should be regarded as a *fourth force* in the counseling profession. The first critical factor in counseling is the *client,* the second is the *counselor,* and the third is the *therapeutic relationship.* Without these, counseling cannot exist.

Some counselors may immediately ask the question, "Should all counselors now train in the culture, values, and norms of different groups of people?" This is surely not a realistic approach. However, counselors should seek to ascertain what the main cultural problem is to be addressed, and what possible solutions are the most practical culturally. The context of the client's assumptions about a helping cure is not only a part of, but forms the core of multicultural counseling.

From a socio-political point of view, because of a different cultural background, it is the right of people of Australia first to own a cultural identity. This includes expressing cultural heritage in the areas of religion and language. The acknowledgement of cultural identity is in direct contrast to assimilation, which assumes that people from different cultural background will abandon their cultural identity. While most people in Australia are satisfied with their lives there is a stark contrast in how people describe their respective cultural identity (e.g., indigenous Australians overwhelmingly call themselves Aboriginal, or Torres Strait Islanders, first). This forms the core of their cultural identity.

Counselor Awareness, Values, and Intentions

Patterns of counselor intentions that appear in counselor research provide evidence that counselors use an integrative mix of both relational and task/technique type intentions. These findings are consistent with relationship-centered counseling theory, which holds, with respect to *personal* and *professional* values, that counselors have a general value system that is high both in relational-humanistic values and task-oriented values.

Thus, it was clear that as counselor I was not detached from the counseling relationship with Sarah, as personal beliefs, values, culture, and attitude play a major role. McLeod (2003, 493) in short puts it this way "important tasks include—being aware of the balance of motives."

Working with Sarah from a Client's Perspective

Although Sarah came to the counseling relationship demoralized, confused, and defeated it did not mean that she was ignorant about what was best for her. As the counseling process started with no preconceived ideas, describing via Sarah's theory how to integrate, was challenging. First, trust in the process of therapy, and second, faith in the resources of the client are necessary prerequisites. From a multicultural counseling perspective I responded to Sarah from a number of content sources, such as specific problems she experienced and specific approaches or solutions she believed in; i.e., her perspective and story emphasizes the following underlying cultural aspects of the client:

- Sarah's concept of reality
- The sense of what it means to her to be a person (sense of self)
- The making of ethical and moral choices, the sense of right and wrong
- Sarah's concept of time

- The significance between Sarah's cultures and her environment

Using self-disclosure during multicultural counseling with Sarah had positive effects. It was a helpful intervention that was used infrequently and judiciously. It was important to be mindful of the content of self-disclosure. Disclosures such as benign biographical data are likely to be well received by clients while they offer little insight in therapy work.

As multicultural counseling does not easily fit into any of the mainstream counseling approaches such as psychoanalytic, person-centered, cognitive-behavioral or systemic counseling, the most appropriate school is an *integrative* approach. While Duncan and Miller (2000) hold the notion that the client is the centre stage, McLeod (2003) departs from the basis that culture is the core element that forms the personal identity. However, one must not overemphasize culture, which could result in undervaluing the person. There seems to be a fine line between the core elements of multicultural counseling as described above and yet, as Nelson (2002, 416) writes, "literature supports a fundamental tenet of the counseling profession; that the relationship between counselor and client is the primary vehicle through which healing occurs."

Research further indicates that multicultural counseling is based on a set of principles, values or beliefs rather than being based on techniques or specific skills. Counselors involved in the practice of this discipline may use different forms of delivery such as individual, couple, family or group counseling, or may employ improvised interventions that are suitable in the presenting problem. Although the client is in a therapeutic relationship with the counselor, consideration is given to cultural appropriate matters.

This specific kind of skill is often referred to as *intentional interviewing*, as the same skills may have different effects on people from varying cultural backgrounds. One specific skill that can be applied in effective multicultural counseling is *willingness to talk about cultural issues.*

A competent and effective counselor will be aware that these specific skills are based on three major paths:

1. Experiential. This approach requires no formal training and many applied counselors who become competent do so through extensive and deep contact with other cultures at a critical period during their lives. They develop a feel and understanding of the sources of human variability that culture provides, and more specifically their own culture.
2. Literature, films, art, music and poetry could allow the counselor to study the phenomena of multicultural counseling in detail and in this way become comfortable and knowledgeable. Academic and scholarly paths are ruled by the vast world of literature and a respectable level of competence could be achieved in this way.
3. Training the counselor may help in foreign counseling situations.

Counseling Action Plan

The counselor's goal. As a practicing counselor, my first and foremost task was to hear Sarah's story and my second to find positive strengths to help her generate a new story. The prime goal is to learn about the client's lived experience. Without Sarah's story it was almost impossible to start any treatment. The aim of treatment is to cultivate the client's *hope* and favorable expectations of getting help.

To focus on cultural issues is not only a goal for counselors, it is also a goal for clients. We were both involved in *mutual goal setting*—we both worked towards where Sarah wanted to go. My goal therefore was to undo the *stuckness* (a term for immobility, incongruence, blocks, and an inability to achieve goals) that Sarah brought to the counseling relationship. There were a variety of reasons for this *stuckness,* and she needed a new story.

Another part of the goal was to get to a stage in the counseling process where Sarah moved beyond denial and anger into a mode of acceptance and recognition of reality. This was achieved through *challenging* her in a supportive fashion, through *listening* for understanding and being culturally empathic. Showing respect for her cultural differences and being sensitive to them showed Sarah that I cared in building towards a trusting relationship. Supportive, empathic confrontation was successful when I clearly listened to Sarah's story. This approach helped her generate her own resolutions. As a goal in the counseling relationship, and with the right *timing,* it helped her overcome demoralisation. Demoralization is a common element and a core problem shared by all clients seeking counseling.

Strategic counseling interventions It is important to note that strategic interventions used by counselors may be at least one discernable component of the therapeutic alliance. The process of client change in a counseling alliance is grounded in the client's readiness to change. There are six strategies, which could be applied by the counselor that may lead to interpersonal influence:

1. Interpretation and reframing Sarah's story
2. Logical consequences of her actions
3. Self-disclosure by the counselor

4. Feedback to Sarah of clear data on her performance
5. Counselor sensitivity about information, advice, opinion and suggestions
6. Directives in creating a new story for Sarah

Parloff (1986) makes reference to four strategies that are commonly implemented during the initial phases of intervention of all counseling and in short describes them as follows:

1. While the counselor shows concern, the client may offer a special type of relationship by disclosing issues that are normally not shared general conversations.
2. Efforts are made to establish an aura in the treatment setting that makes it special.
3. The counselor offers a conceptional schema: an explanation for the client's subjective state.
4. Therapy is based on the client's conceptional schema that offers a prescribed set of procedures and actions.

The use of specific methodology and procedures may provide further evidence of the counselor's knowledge and competence. At the same time these strategies may provide the opportunity to learn that the feared consequences of thoughts and behavior may in fact not occur. Through cognitive and experiential learning opportunities, the client is helped to learn new ways of formulating problems. These opportunities will enhance the promotion and development of a client's self-esteem.

Further research on intervention strategies and approaches suggest that the strongly relational-type intention of *support* stands out as the most highly rated intention that counselors agree on. It also suggests that relationship holds a high place among counselors who practice from a counseling school of integration. Research findings suggest that it is the pattern of using both *common and specific* interventions that best accounted for outcomes, rather than the use of either type of interventions individually.

As in all counseling sessions focused on positive outcomes, multicultural counseling also demands that the counselor evaluates change. In doing so the counselor observes the client's thinking and behavior. The counselor can determine where the client is functioning in terms of change at any time during the therapeutic process. In turn will help to discover how effective the interventions have been.

Daily life and complexities of Sarah's world were such that going home after each session was difficult. Equally difficult for her was to maintain any change in her thoughts, feelings or behavior. Although clients revert to less intentional behaviors, there are some ways to facilitate the transfer of learning from the therapeutic process to daily life. Role-play, imagery exercises, record keeping of behavioral charting and progress notes, homework in the form of tasks, family or group counseling, and follow-up and support by the counselor are some of the most contemporary ways to end a counseling session. These help to ensure that transfer is made. Another way is to integrate into counseling practice a treatment manual, which research has shown to be positive at treatment termination.

Respect. Research literature on treatment effects underscores the important role that client factors play in the outcome of a therapeutic process. Client variables account for the largest portion of variance in counseling change. What Sarah brought into therapy had the most influence on what happened in the treatment. The importance of client factors is underlined when a counselor is empathic, collaborative, and "respectful" of the client's language, cultural, and living context, "this is the best practice."

Trust and therapeutic alliance. Therapeutic success is essentially based on *trust* that the counselor in his or her ability instills through the capacity of connectedness. This connectedness conveys an adequate level of competence to effectively help a client under distress. Session-long intentional support provides a warm empathic environment and increases trust and rapport. It helps the client feel understood and comfortable, and it is ranked highly.

Counseling from the perspective that theories of the treatment of mental illness began to form some new ideas and that transference and pathologically distorted perceptions are no longer assumed to form the core of the interaction between client and counselor. One hypothesis of necessary and sufficient conditions for counseling placed the alliance at the centre of the healing process.

A critical issue in counseling is that the same skills applied by counselors may have a different effect on people with different cultural backgrounds. Diversity and different life experience will always stand out in the mainstream of counseling, and diversity and different life experience are both central to the many issues of multiculturalism. "In effect, all interviewing is multiculturalism," McLeod (2003, 177) states. This perspective is clearly supported by Patterson (2004, 67) in his writing that the seeds of the irrelevance of competencies, with regard to multicultural counseling are found in two early statements: (a) that, "we are all multicultural individuals," and (b) that, "everyone is a multicultural person." Thus there is no specific form, "as all counseling is multicultural."

The big question counselors face about effectiveness of interventions is, what procedures will work for a client, and under what conditions? This is an issue that surely must not be overlooked in multicultural counseling and in Sarah's case, this had been the approach. She was acknowledged as a human being and as a cultural being at the same time.

After coming to know Sarah's story about her feeling lonely she agreed to engage in a group involved in South American cultural art. Sarah reported to have been enjoying their friendship and support to the extent that she later became a member of their leader group. Her social activities grew beyond her expectations after she developed more self-confidence. The last time we talked she mentioned that her general perceptions about Australia had changed. Sarah was excited that she had progressed to the point where she had applied for Australian citizenship. She presented joy. This was expressed in her bubbly face, something that was missing when she attended her first counseling session.

References

Ackerman, S. J., and M. J. Hilsenroth. 2003. A review of therapist characteristics and techniques positively impacting the therapeutic alliance. *Clinical Psychology Review* 23: 1–33.

Beutler, L. E., and T. M. Harwood. 2002. What is and can be attributed to the therapeutic relationship? *Journal of Contemporary Psychotherapy* 32(1): 25–33.

Duncan, B. L., and S. D. Miller. 2000. The client's theory of change: Consulting the client in the integrative process. *Journal of Psychotherapy Integration* 10(2): 169–187.

Horvath, A. O. 2001. The therapeutic alliance: Concepts, research and training. *Australian Psychologist* 36(2): 170–176.

Ivey, A. E., and M. B. Ivey, and L. Gebo. 2003. *Intentional interviewing and counseling.* USA: Phoenix Color Corporation.

Kelly, E. W. 1997. Relationship-centered counseling: A humanistic model of integration. *Journal of Counseling and Development* 75: 337–345.

Kisthardt, W. E. 2001. The strengths perspective in interpersonal helping. In *The strengths perspective in social work practice.* Boston: Allyn and Bacon.

Knox, S., and C. E. Hill. 2003. Therapist self-disclosure: Research-based suggestions for practitioners. *Journal of Clinical Psychology* 59: 529–539.

Larner, G. 2001. The critical-practitioner model in therapy. *Australian Psychologist* 36(1): 36–43.

Lonner, W. J. 1997. Three paths leading to culturally competent psychological practitioners. In *International journal for intercultural relevance,* vol 21. Bellingham.

McLeod, J. 2003. *An introduction to counseling.* Maidenhead: Open University Press.

Menadue, J. 2002. Australian multiculturalism: Success, problems and risks. *Journal of Multiculturalism in Australia* 214: 20–23.

Ministry of Agriculture and Forestry, New Zealand Government. 2002. *Rural Bulletin on Cultural Diversity.*

Nelson. M. L. 2002. An assessment-based model for counseling strategy selection. *Journal of Consulting and Development* 80: 416–421.

Palmer, S., and P. Laungani. 1998. *Counseling in a multicultural society.* Sage Publications.

Parloff, M. B. 1986. Frank's Common Elements in psychotherapy: Non-specific factors and placebos. *American Journal of Orthopsychiatry* 56(4): 521–530.

Patterson, C. H. 2004. Do we need multicultural counseling competencies? *Journal of Mental Health Counseling* 26(1): 67–73.

Rogers, C. R. 1980. *A way of being.* Boston: Houghton Mifflin.

Chapter Thirteen

Do Counselors Require Technical and Scientific Expertise?

To answer the question whether practising counselors require technical and scientific expertise, we need to look at the roles and influences of these two factors within the professional counseling practice. We also need to answer the question whether both technical and scientific expertise are pivotal to deliver effective counseling and successful outcomes.

Defining Counseling

It is important to understand and define counseling as there are as many definitions of counseling as there are theories, models, and practices. Counseling as a separate discipline within the human sciences is much more than something happening between two people. It is an occupation, profession, and a social institution entrenched in multicultural societies and includes the client's theory of change.

The Influences and Demands of Scientists and the Medical Model

Based on counseling therapeutic inadequate outcomes, questions arise whether counseling is effective or has value as a healing enterprise in the field of human services. This perspective of the scientist as well as the influence of the medical school of thought pushes for measurable outcomes and accountability in a field where intangible human function plays a major role.

The emancipation of counseling as a separate discipline within the human sciences is the direct result of evolving new schools of thought. In its evolving process it has indicated growth, not only in numbers but also in advanced training and professionalized bodies such as the establishment, in Britain, of the Standing Council for the Advancement of Counseling (SCAC) in 1971. In 1976, SCAC became the British Association for Counseling (BAC) with a growing membership from 1,000 in 1977 to 8,556 in 1992. In 2001 the BAC was renamed British Association of Counseling and Psychotherapy with some eighteen thousand members. A similar growth trend followed in America with the American Psychological Association for Counseling. Apart from the professional members there is also a great number of people involved in voluntary organizations providing non-professional counseling. Many of them are working in *human services* domains such as nursing, police, teaching, and similar organizations and occupations.

The demand for counseling has manifested itself in a universally accepted method for healing. According to a U.S. news poll 81 percent of respondents agreed that attending a therapeutic session for personal problems would be helpful. A survey done in

Australia has revealed that 79 percent of respondents would be willing to pay for counseling services and that one of the primary roles of a counselor is to help them solve personal problems. Further findings reported by Sharpley et al. revealed that although a great deal of counselor expertise is gained through formal training, the general public displays an expectation that counselors should also have some degree of life experience and reflect a degree of common sense in practice.

Deciding on whether a therapeutic counseling session is beneficial or whether a certain way of working is useful and beneficial to a client brings a new dimension to practicing counseling (Raw 1993). His experience for over twenty years has made him raise questions whether research is beneficial to the practitioner. Raw's main query is whether the information processed by practicing counselors is contained in psychotherapy research, so that it in effect *trickles down* into the field of research and changes and adjusts the character of what counselors do.

Therapeutic treatment methodology has evolved from the Freudian school of positive transference, through the school of necessary and efficient conditions to the collaborative-interactive school of alliance. This alliance between the counselor and the client appears to play an important role in help efforts. Research suggests that the quality of the relationship in the beginning of the process has a significant impact on client retention and outcome of therapy. Further support to this approach is given by Ackerman and Hilsenroth (2003), who maintain that the counselor's *personal attributes* and the use of a *variety of therapeutic techniques* positively influence the relationship between counselor and client.

Research supports the notion that the relational capacity of both parties will have a bearing on the quality of the relationship. Thus, training the counselor to fully utilize and manage this relationship would benefit the process and aid an outcome beneficial to the client.

Evidence that Counseling is Effective and Efficient

That counseling is effective, efficient, and long lasting has been scientifically proven with little evidence of differential effectiveness between schools of therapy. However, there are determining factors that do play pertinent roles in the outcome of therapy. These are referred to as common factors. A study shows that *client variables and extra therapeutic* events have about 40 percent impact on the outcome of a therapeutic session. *Quality relationship* between client and counselor contributes to some 30 percent, while *placebo effects* and *technique* account for about 15 percent each. The debate whether one technique is better than another is continuing.

The lack of clear evidence that counseling is effective is shining a negative light on the credibility of counseling. For the practitioner this has serious implications, but evidence for the effectiveness of specific techniques is accumulating. Jerome D. Frank looked at two hypotheses that could bring positive emphasis to the fore. The first hypothesis is that of *demoralization,* which is the core problem shared by all clients seeking counseling. It portrays a view of the client that does not represent the classical school of illness or mental disorder. The second is that all therapeutic counseling shares common elements and this supports the *common factor* findings.

Beliefs and Feelings

The large number of therapeutic approaches without clear restriction to treatment of problems also raises questions about the effectiveness of the proposed treatment. Each new therapy sees itself as the model of the year and prizes itself to be the one and only method for cure. The question to be answered is, "why are alternative treatments, i.e., those treatments that have not scientifically been approved, seemingly successful?" Some researchers have come to the conclusion that a lack of scientific knowledge by communities as well as aggressive strategic marketing by bogus healers could well be the success behind alternative treatment. An additional contributor in this area is the *will to believe* which is so entrenched among new age supporters.

Similarly, our responses to feelings of pain, disorientation, and many other symptoms that relate to disease are modeled by cultural and psychological factors such as beliefs, expectations, self-serving biases, and deceptions. Some individuals can carry around with them, long after a disease had been cured, a feeling of illness. In many cases people psychologically create a feeling of illness with the absence of a true disease.

With this as the basis, research has found that there are many good reasons why people believe in these bogus therapies. While some diseases are cyclical others run their natural course and people end up in a state of being healed. Others have been misdiagnosed while symptomatic relief can be perceived as being cured. Psychological distortion of reality is another common factor contributing to the belief in alternative healing.

Methodology of contemporary counseling, which is aimed at the subjective and objective factors pertaining to the client or the relationship between the counselor and the client, leans towards help rather than responding to sickness. Of great importance, contemporary counseling is focused on the quality of the relationship with the client. Further support to the person-centered approach in the search for causes to dysfunctional behavior lies in the principles of strengths-based helping. Here the focus is directed positively on the individual's abilities, mental interests, knowledge, and capabilities other than the negativeness or weaknesses of the person. The perceptions and ideas of the client regarding the problem and possible solution are valuable substances to the therapeutic process. Counseling support works on the need of the client and not from the point of view of what the counselor or someone else believes the client may need. However, the language, voice tone, actions taken, and the appliance of mind skills of the counselor are crucial to the outcome of therapy. Self-disclosure (counter-transference) by the counselor is a technique that may encourage the client to disclose (transference) more about him or herself.

Successful Outcomes in Counseling

A client's story presents itself in the vision that the client held at the time when the story was experienced. A story once told as a tragedy or a thriller can become a romance or comedy in another telling. The absence of theoretical content will create an opportunity for the therapist to explore the way that the client experienced the story. The purpose in this approach is to identify the nature and quality of what the person had experienced. This approach is being referred to as *Phenomenology*. In this way the therapist excludes the assumptions he or she holds about the vision or the story that is presented by the client, and tries to describe it in a sensitive but comprehensive manner.

Successful establishment of a relationship of trust between the counselor and the client is imperative. McLeod (2003) compares the congruent person-centered counselor to an *actor* who projects and commits him or herself fully in the relationship with the client and stays engaged for as long as the meeting requires. Periods of authentic encounter between the counselor and the client is where the most meaningful and significant learning takes place. Becvar et al. (2003) describe psychotherapy to be in a conversational domain where the *art* of psychotherapy is a conversational *art*. However, Hayes (2002) is of the opinion that personal unattended hurt from the past in the life of the counselor could handicap counseling as a career. On the other hand, he or she can approach others with honesty, compassion, and humility.

Some theories hold that humans have the inherent capacity to learn, develop, grow, change, and reach for the fulfillment of their own personal selves and their own ideal destinies. Subjective analysis holds the premise that introspection has psychotherapeutic value. The subjective world of emotion is the source for much unhappiness and dysfunctional behavior. Deeply engrained thoughts, perceptions, and personal judgments that can help to unravel the inner-self; it is that side of the person that is not at public display at a time and place when information of inner feeling is required for problem solving. To be able to get into the emotional domain of a client and to stay engaged in the relationship with the client, the counselor as an artist or *actor* comes to a point of decision whether a certain approach is working or not, or whether the counselor has succeeded by using his or her personal skills, warmth, knowledge, and experience.

It is in the division of theory, practice, and research that led to the plethora of theories, therapeutic treatments, and the belief that some are more successful than others. Technical expertise and scientific research highlights the conditions under which the best outcomes can be achieved while it explains the process that connects what we do with the outcomes. There is also the point of view that common and specific effects cannot be separated. Input variables, common interventions, unique interventions, relationship qualities, and the fit of treatment to the client are all interacting aspects of therapy. How these classes of factors interact is complex and must be understood in order to predict and control outcomes.

At the same time we also need to be cautious in our expectations as it all is not as simple as it appears. Research projects undertaken in laboratories do not have the same conditions as those in the field. Specifically funded, single approach, and time-limited projects are often better resourced than real-life situations of the client and the counselor. However, researchers have suggested that counselors can overcome some of these concerns through utilizing laboratory tests in counseling practice. This in turn can encourage field researchers in identifying the features that account for positive outcomes.

Integrating these research results into training programs is paramount in contemporary counseling. Doing so will address the tension the counseling profession struggles with on the understanding of the more intangible, indefinable aspects of human functioning. Failing to make use of technical and scientific expertise may cause serious damage to the counseling profession. Simultaneously it will be creating an opportunity for the *alternative healing* industry to expand. Counselors who inspire to achieve the highest level of treatment should make every effort to stay abreast with empirical findings and the value they have in the counseling discipline. Although a great deal of counselor expertise is gained through formal training, the general public displays an expectation that counselors should also have some degree of life experience and reflect a good degree of common sense.

References

Ackerman, S. J., and M. J. Hilsenroth. 2003. A review of therapist characteristics and techniques positively impacting the therapeutic alliance. *Clinical Psychology Review* 23: 1–33.

Asay, T. P., and M. J. Lambert. 1999. The empirical case for the common factors in therapy: Quantitative findings. In *The heart and soul of change: what works in therapy.* Washington, DC: The American Psychological Association.

Becvar, D. S., R. J. Becvar, P. Quinlin, A. Kennedy, and T. Wahlquist. 2003. *Family Therapy,* 5th ed. USA.

Beutler, L. E., and T. M. Harwood. 2002. What is and can be attributed to the therapeutic relationship? *Journal of Contemporary Psychotherapy* 32(1): 25–33.

Beyerstein, B. L. 1997. Why bogus therapies seem to work. *Skeptical Inquirer* Sept/Oct: 29–24.

Christensen, A., and N. S. Jacobson. 1994. Who (or what) can do psychotherapy: The status and challenge of non-professional therapies. *Psychological Science* 5(1): 8–13.

Duncan, B. L., and S. D. Miller. 2000. The client's theory of change: Consulting the client in the integrative process. *Journal of Psychotherapy Integration* 10(2): 169–187.

Fear, R., and R. Woolfe. 1999. The personal and professional development of the counselor: the relationship between personal philosophy and theoretical orientation. *Counseling Psychology Quarterly* 12(3): 253–262.

Goode, E. E., and B. Wagner. 1993. Does psychotherapy work? *U.S. News and World Report,* May 24: 57–65.

Hayes, J. A. 2002. Playing with fire: Countertransference and clinical epistemology. *Journal of Contemporary Psychotherapy* 32(1): 93–100.

Horvath, A. O. 2001. The therapeutic alliance: Concepts, research and training. *Australian Psychologist* 36(2): 170–176.

Kelly, E. W. 1997. Relationship-centered counseling: A humanistic model of integration. *Journal of Counseling and Development* 75: 337–345.

Kisthardt, W. E. 2001. The strengths perspective in interpersonal helping. In *The strengths perspective in social work practice*. Boston: Allyn and Bacon.

Knox, S., and C. E. Hill. 2003. Therapist self-disclosure: Research-based suggestions for practitioners. *Journal of Clinical Psychology:* 59: 529–539.

Larner, G. 2001. The critical-practitioner model in therapy. *Australian Psychologist.* 36(1): 36–43.

McLeod, J. 2003. *An introduction to counseling*. Maidenhead: Open University Press.

Nelson-Jones, R. 2003. What are basic counseling skills? In *Basic counseling skills: A helpers manual*. London: Sage.

Parloff, M. B. 1986. Frank's Common Elements in psychotherapy: Nonspecific factors and placebos. *American Journal of Orthopsychiatry* 56(4): 521–530.

Raw, S. D. 1993. Does psychotherapy research teach us anything about psychotherapy? *The Behavior Therapist* March: 75–76.

Rogers, C. R. 1980. *A way of being*. Boston: Houghton Mifflin.

Sharpley, C. F., J. E. Bond, and C. J. Agnew. 2004. Why go to a counselor? Attitudes to, and knowledge of, counseling in Australia, 2002. *International Journal for the Advancement of Counseling* 26(1): 95–108.

Wampold, B. E., ed. 2001. Competing meta-models: The medical model versus the contextual model. In *The great psychotherapy debate: Models, methods and findings*. Mahwah, New Jersey: Lawrence Erlbaum.

Chapter Fourteen

Ethics and Morals Integral to Counseling

Ethical and moral issues play important roles in the counseling process of the practicing counselor. There is a continuous demand on counselors to possess an informed awareness of the different ways in which moral and ethical issues may surface in their practice (McLeod 2003). The following two different scenarios illustrate some ethical and moral issues, faced by both the counselor and the client. It is helpful in bringing the focus closer to the reality of counseling practice. Being aware of ethical and moral issues is not always good enough.

Scenario One: Dealing with the Medical Profession

A client self-referred following a serious relationship break-up. I was concerned, as the client presented ongoing psychological problems, including anxiety and panic attacks. I believe these symptoms were exacerbated by medication prescribed by her general practitioner (GP). How could I raise these concerns with the GP? Should I have mentioned these concerns to the client?

A professional approach is the way that the counselor relies on a personal high standard of competence. As a non-medically qualified professional the counselor is perceived to be questioning the treatment plan of the medical practitioner and although it is quite legitimate for the counselor to raise such a concern, it needs to be done in a professional way.

The needed ethical guidelines do not clearly identify the responsibilities of the counselor in a case such as this, neither do they spell out how the counselor should respond. However, counselors must respect the essential humanity, worth and dignity of all people and promote this value in their work. This incorporates the issues of whether the counselor's concerns should be raised with the GP and whether the counselor should mention them to the client.

Whether choosing to contact the GP or not, it is crucial to address the concerns in an objective way, as any criticism could imply inappropriate treatment which is potentially defamatory. Defamation of character as Reamer (2000, 358) states, "occurs as a result of the publication of anything injurious to the good name or reputation of another, or which tends to bring him in disrepute."

Equally important is the knowledge that is used for deliberation about how to achieve ends sought effectively. While this knowledge does not, in this case, relate to the client directly, it does impact the decisions the counselor faces in relation to the client. On the one hand, morally virtuous counselors would need not only to care about helping clients work through their worries and difficulties, but would also need to know how to do so competently. This includes incorporating actions that prevent possible negative consequences. Not being concerned about the consequences, on the other hand, may not impact directly on the client, but may bring harm to the counselor through legal action by the GP. This approach is supported by Cohen and Cohen (1999) in their suggestion that the morally virtuous counselor is more than simply a clever person; he or she knows how to attain the desired target.

All Reasonable Steps are to be Taken to Avoid Harm

In many instances, counselors are faced with problems for which there are not always positive choices. Regardless of the option chosen, some harm may come to the client or counselor in some form or another. In such situations there is the rule of least harm. This rule suggests that the counselor has the opportunity to choose the option that will result in the least harm, the least permanent harm, or the most easily reversible harm. On the one end of the scale, the use of the routine application may diminish the possibility of selecting the most effective intervention technique. But on the other end of the scale there may be times when it is justified to utilize an option that has great risks but which enhances the likelihood of a successful outcome. When opting for such a choice, the counseling plan should be made only with the full consent and agreement of the client.

Treat with Confidence Any Personal Information About Clients

In circumstances similar to this scenario counselors must reconcile conflicting duties and obligations in a way that is consistent with the profession's ethical standards and code of conduct. While Reamer (2000) is of the opinion that to date, counselors have no access to a structured guide that could help them assess their efforts to identify and work on key ethical issues, Parsons (2001) holds the notion that to position oneself as a counselor is not only an academic and intellectual issue, it is a real-life dilemma that has the potential to impair not only on the client but also on the practitioner.

In a contemporary society it is almost impossible to go through counseling without dealing with the question of values. To the counselor this is equally relevant as no therapist can engage in a counseling relationship without bringing certain convictions and values into the helping process.

These convictions may not be specifically mentioned to the client. However, they underline and determine the goals of therapy. Van Hoose and Paradise (1979, 16) state: "Values are attitudes, convictions, wishes and beliefs about how things ought to be." In this contemporary world of counseling the new mentality is a unique ethical cast of mind that is positive and loving within a sphere of seeing people and working with them as persons.

Any consultation with the GP needs to be on professional and confidential basis. Once the relationship with the GP had been established, the client should be informed on the plan of action. All consultation is conducted with the client's consent. Also important is to document the decision-making process, which will reflect critical information pertaining to the client's problem.

Scenario Two: Dealing with Teenagers' Privacy

A parent of a sixteen-year-old teenager who had been for counseling had requested a copy of the child's records. The teenager doesn't want the parent to see the records. Does the parent have a right to see these?

In short, a sixteen-year-old must be treated as an adult and all aspects with regard to privacy and confidentiality must be respected. The counselor is custodian of sensitive personal information of the mature minor. All ethical and responsible decisions are to be made to maintain confidentiality or to disclose client information. The counselor is bound in this role by legal responsibilities and options under common law and statute.

Counselors Are Responsible for Protecting the Client's Rights

It is crucial that a theory pertaining to the rights of people include the fundamental interests of all teenagers. A teenager's integrity, as a person is as significant as his or her rationality, which is built on the dynamic model of children's rights. Teenagers have an autonomy that emerges from their potential capacity for rationality. This dynamic model is based on the approach, which recognizes the autonomy of the *mature minor* in the context of psychological and medical decision-making and the extent of parental authority with respect to the mature minor. The bundle of rights and interests that teenagers have is a reflection of the fact that mature minors are people, although they, for much of their time, remain in a dependent status.

Counselors Treat with Confidence Any Personal Information about Clients

In some cases, access to client confidential records can be gained without the counselor's agreement or discretion. This can be achieved via legally enforced disclosure by solicitors acting for the client's parents in proceedings, both civil and criminal. As counselors do not possess privilege, they must comply with a court order on the basis that the courts require the fullest access to records that may be of evidential value in deciding a case. Confusion, for some counselors, exists about whether a court order applies to *second sets of notes*, meaning notes that are subjective, personal and reflect character rather than more formal objective notes. Unfortunately, all notes in possession of the counselor are to be disclosed under the penalty of contempt of court for failure to comply. In the absence of notes the court can summon the counselor to give evidence in person. This situation illustrates the limitations of any professional practice that does not put client confidentiality in the context of the wider judicial public interest.

Counselors Require the Client's Informed Consent

Although various courts, legislators, and counseling agencies do not always agree on the meanings and applications of informed consent standards, Reamer (2000) is of the opinion that there is considerable agreement about the core elements that counselors should incorporate into consent policies, should there be any possibility of identifying the client. Such policies should include insurances that coercion and undue influence do not affect a client's decision to consent. They should also include the following:

- Clients are mentally capable of giving consent
- Onset to specific procedures or actions are necessary
- Clients are aware that they have the right to refuse or withdraw consent
- Decisions are based on true and adequate information
- Clients are aware that their cases may be discussed with the counselor's colleagues or supervisors

In support of the notion to entrench informed consent policies in one's practice is Corey (1996, 58) who writes that, "one of the best ways of protecting the rights of clients is to develop procedures to help them make informed consent." Providing clients with support that may strike a balance between too much or too little information could allow them to become active participants in the therapeutic relationship. Clients can be overwhelmed if the counselor goes into too much detail initially about the intervention he or she is likely to make. In many cases clients do not realize that they have any rights and do not think about their own responsibilities in solving their problems. It is always a professional approach to provide clients with enough data to make informed choices about entering and continuing the counseling relationship.

The counselor as a professional practitioner should have procedures in place to identify ethics-related-risks, to prevent ethical complaints and possible ethic-related litigation. Practicing counselors should have clearly-worded and comprehensive summaries of client's rights. Such policies and summaries should reflect confidentiality and privacy, release of information, informed consent, access to service, access to records, service plans, service provision, options for alternative service, referrals, the right to refuse service, termination of service and grievance procedures. In tort law (a tort involves a private or civil wrong, from the Latin *tortus* or *twisted*), a risk entails a hazard, danger, peril, exposure to loss, injury, disadvantage, or destruction. The professional counselor is to be aware of these.

The right of the mature minor to prohibit the parents from seeing his or her records must be respected by the counselor. Should there be any parental rights, other public interest, or difficulties in the ability of the sixteen-year-old in decision-making when issues of a psychiatric nature or disability are present, to have access to the records the procedures should be followed via legal routes. A breach of confidentiality in this case would lead to the same sanctions as would apply to breach of confidentiality with regard to an adult.

References

Cambell, T. D. 1992. The rights of the minor. In *Alston, Parker and Seymour*, op cit 1.

Chenoweth, L., and D. McAuliffe. 2005. *the road to social work and human service practice: An introductory text.* InfoTrac.

Cohen, E. D., and G. S. Cohen. 1999. Ethics and virtue. In *The virtues therapist: Ethical practice of counseling and psychotherapy.* USA: Brookes/Cole Publishing Company.

Corey, G. 1996. *Theory and practice of counseling and psychotherapy,* 5th ed. USA: Brooks/Cole Publishing Company.

Freeman, M. 1992. The limits of children's right's In *Ideologies of children's right's: The free press.*

Gillick, V. W. 1986. *The internationalization of children's human rights: Too radical for American adolescents.* Connecticut.

Loewenberg, F., R. Dolgoff, and D. Harrington. 2000. Guidelines for ethical decision making. In *Ethical decisions for social work practice.* Itasca: F. E. Peacock Publishers.

Manning, S. S. 2003. Organization culture: The tangled web of understanding In *Ethical leadership in human services: A multidimensional approach.* New York: Allyn and Bacon.

McBride, N., and M. Tunnecliffe. 2002. R*isky practices: A counselor's guide to risk management in private practice,* 2nd ed. Palmyra: Artproof Printing Company Pty Ltd.

McLeod, J. 2003. *An introduction to counseling.* Maidenhead: Open University Press.

Parsons, R. D. 2001. Ethical conflicts: The system and the interests of others. In *The ethics of professional practice.* Boston: Allyn and Bacon.

Reamer, F. 2000. The social work ethics audit: A risk-management strategy. *Social Work* 45(4): 355–366.

Tribe, R., and J. Morrisey. 2005. *Handbook of professional and ethical practice: For psychologists, counselors and psychotherapists.* East Sussex: Brunner-Routledge.

Van Hoose, W. H., and L. V. Paradise. 1979. *Ethics in counseling and psychotherapy: Perspectives in issues and decision making.* USA.

Chapter Fifteen

Interpersonal Skills in Counseling

Interpersonal skills in counseling have many facets. One such facet is our natural style. It moves us in a certain way as we want to help someone, a friend, a family member, and sometimes someone we have met for the first time. As our natural style does not *work* with everyone it can be developed through training. In the process it will blend with other interpersonal skills and will allow us to be more effective.

We have seen, in a previous chapter, people hold some intangible and indefinable capacities. One such human capacity is empathy. Remember the hairdresser's interest in her client who had being diagnosed with terminal cancer? "I have a client who was diagnosed with terminal cancer. She told me this when she visited me yesterday; I didn't really know what to do or say to her. How should I handle her next time she comes in?" The hairdresser was in the right place at the right time. She was in a position where she could connect, and to connect is a social skill.

But why was the hairdresser interested or concerned about her client? Why did she want to connect? The answer lies within the discovery of *mirror neurons* by Giacomo Rizzolati, an Italian neuroscientist (Goleman 2006). These mirror neurons allow us to grasp the minds of others *through feeling* and not by thinking or reasoning. It is a mental capacity of sharing a moment of *empathic resonance*. It is a link between two brains that connect in emotions only. During such moments people experience each other's feelings. Therefore Goleman (2006, 43) writes, "that we cannot see our minds as so independent, separate and isolated." This moment of emotional resonance can lead to authentic connecting. How many times have we heard someone say, "I should have listened to that little voice on my shoulder," or, "If only I knew that it was God speaking to me?" In some way or form they were aware of communicating with someone they *felt* connected to. The key then is to listen carefully to someone's story, show presence, and give quality attention and time. For those who want to pursue counseling further, the following definitions may be valuable:

Attending behavior: Individually and culturally appropriate visuals, vocals, and body language by the counselor.

Open and closed questions: Open questions often begin with who, what, where, when and why. Closed questions may start with is or are, and expect either a yes or no answer.

Encouraging: In the contexts of a counseling session it means to help the client keep talking.

Minimum encourages: This term refers to head nods, open gestures, and positive facial expressions that show that the interviewer is attentive.

Paraphrasing: Feeds back to the client the core thread of what has been said, thus clarifying comments.

Reflection of feelings: Identifying the key emotions of the client and clarifying affective experience.

Verbal tracking: This is done through *minimum encourages,* guiding the client back to the story.

It is important for practicing counselors to keep abreast with counseling techniques and skills. One way of evaluating one's own counseling interpersonal skills level is to take two separate videos of two separate counseling sessions with the same client. Doing so helps one identify those micro interpersonal skills, which require ongoing practice such as body posture and eye contact, and the elimination of other not-so-good habits, which form over time, such as looking out the window while the client is talking. I did just that: took videos of a client during two separate counseling sessions. Through this I demonstrate a method of skills development. At the same time I reflect on research, evidence, and opinions of those in counseling practice.

The major function of attending behavior is to help the person to tell his or her story while at the same time the counselor reduces talk-time to *attend,* showing the person that one is listening to his or her story. This practice will create positive rapport; it will show interest, awareness, and many more facets of attending. Also related and adding to this scenario is the view of Nelson-Jones (2003) that active listening skills are a combination of both interpersonal communication and skilled intrapersonal mental processing beneficial to the counselor.

One aspect that stood out clearly but with different outcomes was that of the client's theory of change. The outcome in the first interview was somewhat loose and had characteristics of generality without a future plan. In contrast to this, the second interview clearly reflects an outcome, which the client's theory of change allows him the thought that he was in control. When he was confronted with a question about whether he had something more or something else to share, he responded with confidence that he was happy and excited about the future. The client's beliefs about his story served as the framework of the counseling process; it was his story that directed the process and which in turn resulted in the positive outcome. He commented that, "Although I have been diagnosed bi-polar, I feel better about the whole thing now."

The two separate videos showed clearly that I had used two different approaches with regard to greeting and initiating the session. In the first session, I started immediately where we had ended the previous session. In contrast with this, the second session started with a short discussion before asking him to continue with his story. He seemed quite happy with the *door opener* I had used, "The receptionist told me that she had looked after you—it is amazing what a cuppa can do this time of the morning." His response then started the counseling process.

In both sessions there were similarities relating to my attending skills. During both sessions I managed to keep eye contact with the client and noticed how his body language added to his story.

During both sessions both of us were relaxed. However, during the second session there were times when I noticed his discomfort with certain issues, as he was very aware that I was observing, listening, and hearing what he was talking about. Through continuous eye contact I also managed to keep appropriate distance while at the same time was also able to practice silent moments when necessary, in contrast to the first session. When the client got anxious he tended to break eye contact for very short spells and also did so when he was thinking or rephrasing what he was about to share. After watching the second video I noticed that I was indicating my interest to the client in a way that almost mirrored his body language. According to Ivey and Ivey (2003), this is not unusual and was quite noticeable in close-up video pictures of his face and mine. The body language reflected by us both made me *consciously* aware of time when I should not interrupt his conversation at all. Smiling appropriately had kept the conversational momentum going. Moments of silence created the chance for him to give more critical information.

Being aware of a difference in our English accents, I consciously tried to speak slower than I do in normal life conversations. This allowed me to be more clearly understood. Therefore my vocal tone and vocal qualities were as constant and identifiable as possible to ensure that the reaction to him was beneficial to the counseling process. I noticed that during both sessions, when I spoke softer I was often requested to repeat the question, although this did not seem to affect the interview. Nevertheless I believe it is good to prepare myself to be in conditions where sound is as clear as possible.

In the first session I stayed with the client's story wherever it led. The second session was different. Here I practiced *verbal tracking*. This was done through *minimum encourages* which enabled me to guide the client back to the story when he was deviating from it. By using the last word of the client's previous sentence it was possible to keep on track. In doing so I felt in control of the process while the client reflected that he was in control of his situation. As I was selective in drawing attention to certain topics I was able to direct the client back to the main story. At the same time, unlike in the first session, I was much less verbally interrupting while the client was talking. This made sure that I obtained the information that was critical. Practice over time will enable counselors to focus on relevant topics more clearly.

During both sessions the aim was to listen to the client's story, to allow him to experience a counseling setting wherein he felt safe and secure, knowing that what he was about to disclose would be handled as confidential. Listening, following the story, and asking fewer questions were more evident during the second session. Open questions starting with what, when, where, or how may help the client to say more than only answering with a *yes* or *no*. Such questions posed to the client resulted in him giving more information while he was elaborating on specific details pertaining to his story. It was noticeable how freely the client wanted to talk more after open questions were put to him and how specifically he answered closed questions during both sessions. Although open and closed questions help to bring out the client's story they also help to create a specific and concrete picture of the client's world. Ivey and Ivey's (2003, 76) model question is "Could you tell me a specific example?" This is more valuable in situations where clients tend to remain vague and speak in general terms.

I summarized each interview by giving the client a review about what was understood to be key and selective concepts regarding his story. His positive response, both verbally and through body language, confirmed my check that he understood and accepted my summary. In hindsight, in both interviews I could have summarized key issues more accurately and even more often. Summarizing can be very valuable at the beginning of a session if it is a follow-up from a previous session, at the end of a session, even midway during an interview.

What is also evident and similar in both sessions during the process is my natural style, sitting back and relaxed. It reflects a sense of being comfortable with the client's situation and a willingness to go with what is in the room. It seems to create an atmosphere for natural conversation. However, be aware that every client will be different in approach, personality, and will have a different story. There also appears to be basic natural skills surfacing during the counseling process, which are described as being fundamental and primary rather than advanced.

Having discussed and compared differences and similarities between the two videos, relating to two interviews with the same client again, allowed me to explore the areas of my understanding of the counseling process. It also brought about more detailed understanding of attending skills and the important roles these skills play in counseling. Although there were many differences and contrasting issues between the two sessions there were also many similarities that have been discussed. I found that I followed the client's story more easily during the second session by being a listener rather than wanting to lead the client through asking many questions. However, I believe there are a number of areas for development such as staying with the train of thought of the client. Also critical for successful outcome is the ability to prevent the client going on the defensive. Although I was aware that in both cases the client acknowledged that he had been heard, the *real* difference lies in careful listening.

References

Goleman, D. 2006. *Social intelligence: The new science of human relations.* New York: Bantam Dell/Random House.

Ivey, A. E., and M. B. Ivey. 2003. *Intentional interviewing and counseling.* USA: Phoenix Color Corporation.

Nelson-Jones, R. 2003. *Basic counseling skills: A helpers manual.* London: Sage.

Chapter Sixteen

How Do I Connect?
What Can I Do?

Not all people have the social skills to spontaneously interact with even their neighbors. Yet once they have connected, they become good friends. Not taking the step to make contact appears to be the true hurdle. We can interact in many different ways. I have learned from close friends that after caring for their neighbors' puppy for a weekend, friendship developed. Do we really need an international "neighbor day" so we can interact neighborly one day out of a year? Surely not!

Sometimes a local or national disaster affords a good way of socially interacting. The networking among people and service providers in the process of helping people involved in national disasters is enormous, yet very satisfying. Being involved in setting up contingency plans for national disasters is but only one area of pre-counseling in another form. During the Bali-bombings a number of trauma counselors were on the ground meeting survivors on their way home in Australia. Through community networks these counselors were able to connect survivors with their loved ones. This reconnecting with loved ones was psychologically the most precious thing they could have being going through.

Another way to connect is to take the step and get involved in community, church, and similar initiatives and activities. I was surprised by the number of voluntary activities in my neighborhood. It was only when I paged through the local directory, weekly paper, and daily advertising mail that I learned about the various things on offer. I then narrowed my interest down to those services I was interested in. There were still many choices.

Community service needs range from general customer service at your local information centre to alcohol and drug abuse support at the local community center. There is a continuous need for volunteers to give support services in schools and libraries. If you live on the coast or close to a local pool, what about being a volunteer lifeguard? This is where the opportunity lies to change our lifestyle moving away from the big "I" to a community-based environment. As a friend once said to me, "It is hard to find an 'I' in 'we.'"

Finally, there is a need by those who want to connect personally. This was the story of the hairdresser. She was in a position where she felt connected, where she was experiencing emotional resonance with her client's need for sharing a moment of her inner self. This was a moment so far removed from the hustle and bustle of the world yet so easy to be missed by many. However, in this case the hairdresser was aware of this dance of emotional messages between her and her client. It was empathy, the nurturing of mirror neurons, which prompted her to raise the question "how should I handle her next time she comes in?" Not only did the hairdresser go through a special moment attending to her client's hair, she moved another step closer to experience the feelings and inner world of a person, a person who also sometimes needs to attend to her hair.

About the Author

J ames de Beer was born in Tzaneen, a small town in the north-eastern part of South Africa. In 2000, his family moved to New Zealand, and he is currently living and working in Queensland, Australia.

For the past thirty years James de Beer has dedicated his skills, knowledge, and experience to the field of human services. He served in the South African Police for six years and then joined the South African Defense Force, where he reached the rank of lieutenant colonel. With a growing interest in community, and more specifically with people and relationships, he moved into the area of organization development with intermediate sessions counseling executives who were bringing their private psychosocial problems to the workplace.

After gaining his qualifications and lecturing on military law, he received his BA degree at the University of Pretoria, Republic of South Africa and his Master of Counseling degree at the University of Queensland, Australia.

His first written contribution was as a coauthor on "Poverty and Disability in Australia" published in World Poverty in October 2007. This was a module in the book released by Franciscan International, a representative of the UN in Geneva.

As a family man, James de Beer moved towards a special interest in family and relationship dynamics which included individual and group counseling. He currently practices family, relationship, and individual counseling from an integrative therapy perspective. He has a special interest in helping people live healthier lifestyles with the purpose of creating healthy communities.